Spiritual
Numerology
Caring for Number One

Spiritual
Numerology
Caring for Number One

To Gaye: May this book help you to greater unity with The One. — David Pitkin

by **David J. Pitkin**
(David James)

Illustrations by Roger Mock

Aurora Publications
Ballston Spa, New York

Aurora Publications
P.O. Box 387
Ballston Spa, New York 12020

Library of Congress Cataloging-in-Publication Data
Pitkin, David J. 1939-
Spiritual Numerology: Caring for Number One
ISBN 0-9663925-1-5
Library of Congress Catalog Card Number: 99 096347

Cover: The Orion Nebula Photo credit: NASA

Thomas Merton quote prior to Numbers as Lessons from NEW SEEDS OF CONTEMPLATION, Copyright 1961 by The Abbey of Gethsemani, Inc., Reprinted by permission of New Directions Publishing Corp.

Edgar Cayce Readings
Copyright Edgar Cayce Foundation
1971,1993,1994,1995
Used by permission

Toward the Unknown Region

By Walt Whitman (1819-1892)

Darest thou now O soul,
walk out with me toward the
unknown region,
where neither ground is for the
feet nor any path to follow?

No map there, nor guide,
nor voice surrounding, nor touch of
human hand,
nor face with blooming flesh, nor
lips, nor eyes, are in that
land.

I know it not O soul,
nor dost thou, all is a blank
before us,
all waits undream'd of in that
region, that inaccessible
land.

Till when the ties loosen,
all but the ties eternal, Time
and Space,
nor darkness, gravitation, sense
nor any bounds bounding us.

Then we burst forth, we float,
in Time and Space O soul,
prepared for them,
equal, equipt at last, (O joy! O
fruit of all!) them to fulfil
O soul.

Contents

What am I? I am myself a word spoken by God. Can God speak a word which does not have any meaning? Yet am I sure that the meaning of my life is the meaning God intends for it? Does God impose a meaning on my life from the *outside*, through event, custom, routine, law, system, impact with others in society? Or, am I called to *create from within*, with His grace, a meaning which reflects His truth and makes me His "word" spoken freely in my personal situation? My true identity lies hidden in god's call to my freedom and my response to Him.

Thomas Merton, *Contemplative Prayer*

Foreword

As a new millennium dawns, the opportunities and the perils for humankind are expanding. There seems to be greater personal control over life available to affluent westerners. In the early 1980s President Reagan designated the remaining years of the century as "The Age of the Individual." But the widespread illusion of personal control has increasingly led us to loosen the bonds that formerly gave cohesion to our society. Many accept the assumption that America can remain the world leader, while its people are ignorant of both of the outer world and the inner self. The young are led to believe they can entirely "personalize" their lives and find lasting happiness with only superficial involvement in their neighbors' lives.

More and more, personal gratification is emerging as a primary goal in western societies, and among the elites of non-western nations who can afford to participate. Large social institutions that formerly offered a measure of personal security and societal harmony are weakening. The grand illusion of the physical world, that individuals can live by and for themselves, sustained primarily by possessions and affectation, is nearing full bloom. We *seem* able to find happiness behind our designer facades, without the bother of investigating our inner realities.

Visionaries have spoken for several decades about a "new age" in human affairs–a virtual heaven on earth. And many think this jubilee has arrived. Under a thin veneer of millennial spirituality, hucksters and commercial interests co-opted the movement's idealism to ensure that the old gods of Mammon remain as the deities of a new century. As more and more young adults prostrate themselves before the god of hedonism, the common sense and spirit of critical inquiry that sustained our ancestors during more difficult times in the past, have been abandoned.

While the Pied Piper of Personal Pleasure entices the masses, there are some who have developed an immunity to his seductive tune. Many individuals once under the thrall of self-gratification have discovered, often through great personal suffering, that the personal self is an idol with feet of clay. Dr. Carl Jung deemed the persona (our "walkin' around face") a false god, and noted its diabolical side. His works are enjoying a revival of interest and study among those jaded by materialism. Jung believed that we ignore our spiritual side at our own peril.

How can Modern Man reconnect to the soul's realities when traditional religion seems hoary? Many people, no longer content to seek truth through a single religion, are formulating a "mix and match" spirituality, confounding traditional denominations. The concept of a personal spirituality, as distinct from membership in a formal religion, has attracted the young for over thirty years. Eastern religions, likewise, have made inroads in western thought and religious practice. Even mainline religions are examining ancient, non-western spiritual disciplines (e.g. yoga, the Enneagram or maze walking) not formerly a part of their spirituality or worship.

There is a widespread *hunger* in the world for a connection to That Which Does Not Pass Away, by whatever name It is called. Like an iceberg, whose greater mass is submerged beneath the waters, this appetite for inner peace and meaning has not yet become fully conscious. This famine gnaws away quietly in the unconscious minds of millions, surfacing suddenly in individual lives.

The information explosion, now burgeoning through the electronic media, offers seekers and sufferers many options. But, a crucial question is this: will all the seeking for information become just intellectual exercise, or will it be *used*–creating stronger new institutions and organizations that enable us to find more abundant lives? Will the new spirituality become mere superficial social conversation, or will it strengthen the hearts and souls of many people, enabling them to emerge as helpers and healers of society?

The New Age is dawning with heavy commercial emphasis, threatening to sidetrack genuine spiritual opportunity with baubles and trifles that simply gratify the old afflicted self. Superficial adornments are almost always preferable for the ego, so that it isn't forced to forsake its old defenses. Meaningful growth is possible only for those willing to change their *inner* person. And if we are to rework *that*, we need to examine our inner self more closely, perhaps in ways we have never before attempted.

A tantalizing concept from the ancient wisdom (or perennial wisdom, as some call it) is that our "heaven" lies *within* each person. Therefore, it cannot be purchased or bestowed on us by some other individual. Yet, how can we access this inner world without our old ego defenses controlling the search? Dr. Martin Luther King, Jr. once said that humans love darkness rather than the light. Because they have chosen to live in fear, many people do not *want* to know their personal truth. Today's seekers need to comprehend a fundamental of psychology, that humans are capable of generating *both* Light and Darkness within ourselves.

As the concept of reincarnation gains adherents among western spiritual seekers, and as individuals seek for the causes of global and personal disasters, we may profit by mythologizing about causation. The ancient concept of numerology offers one technique for forming and testing hypotheses about the experiences of individuals. Numerology is not essentially rational, so it offers the opportunity to bypass some of the old logic we have leaned on to explain our life experiences.

While each ancient civilization had its unique analytical system, assigning certain meanings to numbers, *this* book is a product of the dawning Aquarian Age. The author has intuited *a system* for understanding the spiritual motivations within people. It is not the *only system*—only *one* technique that can shed light on the great variations in human experience. While it diagnoses, it also prescribes psychologically sound behaviors that can result in greater personal wholeness.

What is more personal than the name given us at birth? Our name establishes our uniqueness, but also offers us psychic or spiritual connection to those of that name who preceded us in the earth. While given to us by our parents, through their free choice, most numerologists believe that *we* chose our parents for (among many other factors) the name they were destined to give us. While naming seems random, it is anything but. The soul knows what it needs to accomplish during the brief opportunity called "life." Operating in our unconscious, it moves powerfully to accomplish *its* ends, despite the foolishness of the conscious self or persona.

Spiritual Numerology: Caring for Number One offers seekers the opportunity to suspend "sensible" attempts at self-understanding, and a chance to experience a world where numbers are values, but not amounts. Though it uses simple mathematics for computation, the self-analysis that it promotes is not rational or left-brained. It encourages imagination, reflection and an opportunity to explore the wisdom in symbols.

The author has found Truth in all the world's great religions, as each one resulted from some person's attempt to find connection to divinity. The word "religion" derives from the Latin *re ligio*, or attempt to re-connect the individual to the Source from which all life came. The author believes that world religions emerged, and will continue to emerge, wherever and whenever a significant group of people evoke a seeking for Truth. Truth is One, but it has many facets. Cultural or personal interpretations and practices can differ in approaching that Truth, causing groups to forget that there is but *one* Source.

Included in this material is a measure of the philosophy of Edgar Cayce (kay'-see)(1877-1945) whose work has deeply inspired the author, and helped him make sense of the traditions of many world religions. As America's most gifted psychic, Cayce left behind a large amount of transcribed material that members of all religions find inspiring. He urged followers not to make him and his work into idols, but to apply his work in whatever religion or organization they were currently in. His role was to help usher into the earth a more profound human consciousness, so that we might apprehend what The Source desires for us as individuals and as groups.

This book seeks to shed Light where there is Darkness. Over a century ago Victor Hugo wrote:

> *If the soul is left in darkness, sins will be committed. The guilty one is not he who commits the sin, but he who causes the darkness.*

Spiritual Numerology has evolved gradually over a quarter century, arising from the author's prayers to know how he might be useful to The Creator. May it serve to move the reader a bit closer to The Light.

...astrology and numerology and symbology are all but the gateways or the signs of expression.

These, then are as indications; and not other than the signs of things, that may be altered ever by the force or factor from which they emanate.

As related to individuals these each vibrate to certain numbers according to their name, their birth date, their relationships to various activities. Then when these appear, they become either as strengths or as losses or as helps or as change, or as the spiritual forces. But, as indicated, they are rather as the signs, or the omens; and may be given as warnings, may be given as helps, may be given in any manner that they may be constructive in the experience of the individual.

Edgar Cayce

Reading #261-15

Preface

At a *Search for God* Study Group meeting in 1974 my new friend Betty approached me and asked, "David, what is your full birth name and date of birth?" When I supplied these, she scribbled the information onto a note pad and consulted a book that she had held under her arm. Then she began to enumerate the main spiritual issues that I knew I was struggling with. "Betty," I said, "you can't *do that*!" But the fact *was*, she was doing it, and I wanted to know how. Sometime later I borrowed her book and skimmed through it, enough to understand that numerological computation involves assigning number values to the letters of the alphabet.

The whole process seemed too arbitrary and unscientific to me. How can one derive meanings from a name given to us by our parents? In America numerologists assign the number values 1-9 to letters in a 26-letter alphabet, but how about other languages and alphabets? I never got around to solving that one, as I was swept up in discovering a workable system for the English alphabet. Immediately I became immersed in working out the numbers for everyone in my family, and began to see similar numbers or lessons shared by my loved ones. But who is to say just what specific meanings should be attributed to THREE or EIGHT or TWO? Who is to be the final authority?

One of my students told me of a rabbi in Albany, New York, who had recently spoken on numerology to the Saratoga Springs Hadassah. I contacted him for more insight. But the rabbi noted that I was neither Jewish nor literate in Hebrew, and these factors would preclude my full understanding of the Jewish Cabala numerology. He could only urge me to "look beneath the surface" of peoples' names. Within a few days I discovered an injunction in Edgar Cayce's work, to a seeker (in Reading 261-14) for validation of spiritual meaning in numbers:

...we will see these are but signs. Study in some of these, but *turn most to the influence of the force of the One within self.*

If I understood him correctly, Cayce was urging me to an inner search for the truth in these matters, something I believed myself incapable of doing. The American education system has traditionally seen pupils as "empty," and in need of "filling" by some authority. Other than in art, poetry or literature, students are seldom urged to seek intuitive answers but, instead, to depend on rational "truths" prescribed by authorities and traditional methods. The more I studied Cayce, the more I understood that The Christ was not just an historic figure, but also a liberating consciousness which brings Truth to enlighten seekers *within ourselves*. My traditional religious teachers of that time were highly suspicious of seeking higher truths in this manner. I recognized, at the same time, my strong dependency on others' scholarship, because (as a public school teacher) I needed to "fit into" society.

I was recovering from a 1973 bout with cancer at that time and, not knowing how much time remained in my life, the urge to know *my* personal truths outweighed my customary inertia. How does one learn to *hear* or *see* the message in numbers? And how can one know if such messages are accurate and valid? The distillation of my intuitions can be found in the pages of this book. As Cayce urged, I took each new insight "to the streets," so to speak. If there were any truth in my musings, it would have to emerge in offering my insights to others, and in noting their reaction to my explanations.

By 1975 I was hand writing two and three page "readings" for family, friends and co-workers. At first, my almost mechanical procedures offered advice that was brief, if generally accurate. Then, at some point in my work of helping others, I began to gain intuitive insights as I worked on the numbers for those I wanted to help. When attempting to offer constructive assistance to others, I began to understand priorities, or an "order of transformational work" necessary within each person over the present lifetime. My desire then, as it is today, was to assist individuals to be "in the world, but not *of* the world." I also came to understand, within myself, the many illusions that hamper those who desire to be "good."

At the urging of my friend, Agnes, I began to incorporate small amounts of astrological information into the charts that I wrote. Though I studied astrology on the side, I was hoping to avoid the tedious details that seemed necessary in learning, then explaining, such principles in my numerology readings. But Agnes was persistent in her advocacy, and I *was* beginning to see the wisdom of combining the two approaches. Eventually I evolved a system that I termed "Astro-Numerology," which allows deeper understanding of the client through the use of both techniques. My changed attitude was motivated by the desire to provide deeper personal understanding to those I was serving.

By the 1980s I was typing reports of almost twenty pages in length for clients. One day, in the midst of my musings on one person's difficulties, an inner "screen" illuminated in my mind, offering a scene of people in old-fashioned dress from some past time. I wondered if this scene represented my client in a prior lifetime, offered to me for understanding as to where and how the present difficulty arose. Again, I had to confront my inner fear of reproach for providing "wrong" information. But the stimuli continued unabated: words and pictures came to me intuitively with greater frequency.

One night, in the midst of doing a chart for my friend Ann, I heard a woman's jocular voice call out, "That's right. Go get 'em Annie!" Quickly I scanned the room where I was working, but I was the only one there. For better or worse I incorporated the phrase in my writing, and was pleasantly surprised when Ann appreciated the inspiration. I was invited to be a regular guest on Sandy Adams' "Speak Up" talk show on WWSC-AM in Glens Falls, NY, an activity for which I adopted the professional name of "David James," which I have used throughout my numerology career. My work with Sandy lasted several years.

In the midst of another woman's reading I "saw" a small group wearing sixteenth century dress gathered in study in front of a fireplace. As I "looked" at each individual I could understand their psychological issues. I found I could "ask questions" and "receive answers" about the scene. The woman in the center of the group had joined the religious study group (upon "asking" their identity, I was told "Hutterites") to please her husband. But, at the time of this scene, his devotion was weakening as *she* was dedicating herself totally to Hutterite doctrines and practice. I heard the name "Arabella," so I asked for her family name. I got "Berger," which sounded too Germanic for what I perceived as being in the modern Czech Republic. Nevertheless, I put it all down.

When my divorced client responded to the almost thirty page document I sent her, she was ending membership in the second of two churches that had consumed much of her life. She was angry with "controlling and political" church leaders and the duplicity in seeming "spiritual" people. She expressed amazement because her pet name for her daughter in this life is "Arabella." While this incident *proves* nothing, the material I provided to her (and hundreds of other clients over the years) did lead her to introspection about her present-life thought and behavior patterns.

In 1989, understanding that my teaching days were numbered (no pun intended), I sought a Masters degree in Counseling Psychology at Goddard College in Plainfield, Vermont. I hoped this preparation would allow me not only to identify (through numerology) a person's spiritual issues, but also permit me to offer sound psychological advice as to therapies for their present difficulty. I thought the degree would lead me to become a formal counselor who used numerology in therapeutic analysis. Many times my advice was for clients to seek a good counselor or therapist to assist their healing. My thesis at Goddard involved blending my spiritual numerology insights with studies in Developmental Psychology.

At the start of each school year, I asked my ninth grade students to fill out data cards to help me understand the nature of the mind and soul I was instructing. Most students never knew that I had their numerology done by October and (for many of them) I made a quick astrological "solar chart" in the card's margin. Teachers receive over one hundred different personalities and souls on the opening day of school, and are told "teach them," as if learning is possible without allowance for individuality. Few teachers, I suspect, have as much potential insight into the students' inner world as I had. When it seemed advisable (i.e. when I believed I wasn't violating beliefs of the few students who have religious homes today) I would bring the data card to personal conferences or help sessions with students. Many teens responded positively to the concept of their potential unique role in the world's development. My efforts seem to have helped stimulate many of them as they have grown into wonderful, helping adults.

During our study of Asia (the course was African and Asian Culture Studies, required for graduation by the NY State Social Studies syllabus) I was able to assist some students who had begun a search for personal meaning. Our textbook noted that many families in India make astrology charts (which become important when parents later arrange the child's marriage) upon the birth of each child. Most teenagers think astrology is simply a column in newspapers or magazines; few had ever seen a personal natal chart. I offered to get computer-made charts for any student who wished one. I also interpreted the charts for those who seemed *seriously* interested. During this process I often wondered how my own life might have been different if I had had a teacher like me.

In the early 1990s I was selected to share my intuitions with conferees at the Association for Research and Enlightenment's annual Intuition Conference in Virginia Beach, Virginia. At an evening lecture I suggested several numerology techniques (from my system) that psychologists or counselors in the audience could use to immediately "size up" new clients. Several of them tried the methods and found them to be useful tools in their therapeutic practices. This was especially rewarding to me, as my personal path did not lead to a formal counseling practice. My personal natal astrology suggests I have other work to do.

In 1994 I teamed up with fellow study group member Bill Getz to offer spiritual retreats and workshops. The former Director of Training at the New York State Education Department, he was experienced in "action planning" that helped state employees maximize their abilities by setting a single inspirational focus in their labors. We merged our programs and began offering workshops and weekend retreats throughout the U.S. and Canada. Our unique program allows individuals to identify and study personal spiritual potential, then develop this inspiration by setting a single spiritual ideal for their lives. [1]

Typing about forty readings a year since the late 1970s, as well as the typing work in my teaching career, has left me with sore wrists and hands. As you will note when using this book's system on *my* name, I have some "balance issues" in taking care of my own physical body. Today, I seldom type full-length charts for others. Instead, I offer this book and system to interested individuals as a starting place in the search for the Self. And I encourage each reader wishing to offer helpful advice to others to *seek for answers within self.*

Begin where I began in 1974. Using my system, make a chart for yourself. Then decipher the purported issues for *your own* life. Test these hypotheses. If you find some validity in this effort, use the system to help others or enhance your understanding of them. Add *your own* insights to my literature. You didn't enter the present life to become just another David. Listen to your intuitions while making and analyzing the charts. *Apply* what you learn. This is only *one* system for understanding your soul's goals.

Edgar Cayce said that we are *all* psychic, because "psychic" refers to *the soul and its eternal purposes.* We *all* have the potential to develop soul powers. While e.s.p. may not be your gift, there is something for you to give to society. Our progress seems greatest when we integrate *service to others* with our personal physical, mental and spiritual development. The Master told us that *we* would do greater works than He had done, because He went to The Father.

None of us knows how far or how fast our personal development may take us. Speed and quantity are just not that important in the spiritual world, but *quality is.* All we need do is begin where we are right *now.* In the words of Al Jolson, "Folks, you ain't seen *nothin'* yet!"

David J. Pitkin
(David James)
Ballston Spa, New York
February 2000

---

[1] For more information: Write Bill Getz, RD#2, Box 180, Schoharie, NY 12157 or e-mail BGETZIDEAL@aol.com.

Making a Numerology Chart

If there is any "truth" in numerology you must discover it first in a personal self-analysis. Once you have become familiar with this process of self-study, then you will be able to work with others' charts with more confidence. There are two charts to make, and they only require that you do your computations correctly. Before reading my analysis of the lesson number that you arrive at, go through your addition a second time, being sure that your total is accurate, and so that you don't waste time studying a number that really is not "yours."

Each of your birth certificate names mythically contains an indication of the work your soul intends to do in this lifetime. On a clean piece of paper, lay them out something like this:

MARY

ANN

THOMAS

Then, use the chart below to substitute a number for each of the letters in your names:

1	2	3	4	5	6	7	8	9
A	B	C	D	E	F	G	H	I
J	K	L	M	N	O	P	Q	R
S	T	U	V	W	X	Y	Z	

Mary Ann's chart, at this stage will look like this:

MARY
4 1 9 7, and then add these digits, 4+1+9+7=21

ANN
1 5 5, and add these digits, 1+5+5=11

THOMAS
2 8 6 4 1 1, and add these digits, 2+8+6+4+1+1=22

To fully understand each lesson, you need to add the digits to one another, until they reduce to a single number. With the 21, for example, we add 2+1 to get her lesson of 3. MARY is a 3 lesson. Sometimes in adding two digits (ex.28, 2+8=10, 1+0=1) you will need to do addition twice in order to reach the single digit.

But, let's look at the 11 and 22 here. Or, using your own name, you may have a 33 or 44 on your sheet. These "**double numbers**" are known by various names. I just call them "double numbers," but some numerologists call them "Power Numbers" or "Master Numbers." Suit yourself. The issue here is that there is mythically something *special* about these numbers, so when we reduce an 11 (1+1=2) it is important to retain the double number too. Thus, 11 will be expressed as 11/2, 22 becomes 22/4, 33 becomes 33/6, and 44 becomes 44/8.

With Mary Ann, then, our chart will read:

M A R Y
4+1+9+7=21=   2+1= 3

A N N
1+5+5=1+5+5=   11, or 11/2

T H O M A S
1+8+6+4+1+2=   22, or 22/4

At this point we begin to suspect Mary Ann is something special, having two double numbers in her name. How these numbers differ from single digit lessons will be explained later, but we can note here that the double numbers entail much greater effort, and require a willingness to strip yourself of illusions that most of the people around you hold onto tenaciously. Mythically, these are life lessons that are derived from the parts of the birth name. **Life Lessons** are lessons that you may or may not have been very successful with in former lifetimes, but which now *do* require much attention. Your soul has moved them to center stage for this lifetime, and you can see these as such in Mary Ann's new personal myth.

Let's continue this chart by adding her three life lessons: 3+2+4=9, or we can add the double numbers too: 3+11+22=36, 3+6=9. I call this total of the entire name, "**the Atmosphere Lesson**" in one's life. It is possible to have a double number or a single one here. Write it down. The "atmosphere" of one's life is a theme that persists between birth and death-a lesson the soul has chosen to struggle with during *each day* of its physical life. An atmosphere may be a set of conditions that surround us, or it may be like the air we breathe in. Deep-sea divers create special atmospheres or gases to help them cope with the great depths. "Breathe in" can also be translated as "in spire." And this, I think, may be the *challenge* function of our atmosphere lesson-to inspire us or to "keep our feet to the fire" during this incarnation, so our soul work can be accomplished.

It is also instructive to see what numbers *do not* appear in the birth name. "**Missing numbers**" are said to represent lessons failed or avoided in former lifetimes. Many times these same digits can appear as one of the life lessons in some component of our name. And they may also appear as the Destiny or Success Lessons.

When a "missing number" does appear as one of our special numbers, we need to pat ourselves on the back (briefly) because it is a representation that our soul has found the courage to attempt a particular activity in this life, which it has formerly been unable to accomplish. Note, for example, that our friend Mary Ann is missing a 3 in her birth name, but has chosen (unconsciously, as a soul) to face it in the sum total of MARY. Mythically, this soul has chosen to transform itself by facing 3 issues in this life. In most individuals, I believe, there is evidence of the soul's attempt to reorient itself by taking on the ***double number version*** of that single digit, obviously raising the stakes for this work. It shows strong determination on *the soul level* to succeed in these issues in the present life.

In this way we can make some guesses about the depth of determination in the unconscious or soul's mind. We must treat missing numbers as mythical "weaknesses at birth." We are obliged to work on them, but we must understand that we are likely to experience difficulty in these attempts. We must not condemn our self for what appear to be "failures," when we have really been trying to improve and grow, but have not yet reached our goal. Persistence is important in struggling with these issues. All we need to do is pick ourselves up just one more time than we have "fallen."

If you have each of the numerical values (1-9) in your birth name letters, the myth is that you have had adequate positive experience with each of the nine areas in past lives. Therefore, in this lifetime, *you* will have experience with lessons 1-9 again, with the hope of strengthening your knowledge and abilities. More is expected of *you* spiritually. Having all the lesson numbers, your soul is mythically seeking to be "well rounded." You will thus have number *cycles* 1-9 in your name (see chapter on Numbers As Cycles).

When you opened this book you had already experienced plenty of suffering in life. And you probably have tried all the popular and "easy" ways to avoid life's pain. Otherwise, you would not be reading self-help books or seeking new, disciplined paths of living. Over 2,000 years ago Siddhartha Gautama, The Buddha, said that life is suffering, most of it brought on by our present or past desires and attachments in the material world. Though we may wish he were wrong, if the soul *has* chosen our present name and incarnation period in history, perhaps there *is* virtue in struggling with the lessons in our chart. This chart represents our "battle plan" for the present life opportunity.

There is a way we might discover our soul's deepest desire before it chose the complicated and unique ingredients of this life. To find

this information, the **Destiny Lesson** or **Destiny Number**, we turn
to the full date of birth. Our friend Mary Ann was born on October
1. 1950. We add these digits together, just as we did with the numbers in her birth name. And we take care to state the year of birth
with all *four* digits:

$$1+0+1+1+9+5+0=17, \; 1+7=8$$

In our workshops, my partner Bill and I simply say, "She is an 8."
This number mythically represents *the soul's greatest urge in enter-
ing this earth* life, an event that is sure to be filled with distasteful
experiences as we undergo our transformation. You may find that
your own **Destiny Number**, as I call it, is a double number. Some
numerologists use different terms for this total: The Life Path or
Soul Path. I prefer *"Destiny"* because it indicates that the soul
intends to do this work and is moving deep in our psyche to achieve
this goal. Until this path is made conscious, however, our ego/con-
scious mind usually doesn't have a clue how *our* life should differ
from others'. So, in our insecurity, we take refuge in trying to blend
into society–to be like "everybody else."

The last number of note is that of our *day* of birth. I call this the
Success Number. It represents a lesson or lessons that we need to
undertake (perhaps as a primary lesson or a work we need to involve
ourselves in) if we are to *succeed* at the Destiny Lesson. Mary
Ann's Success Number is a 1, as she was born on the 1st of October.

The next step in formulating your chart should now be to state
your soul's life plan unemotionally, in the dry language of numbers,
before looking up the potential meanings of the numbers, and
becoming ego involved in how to write it down. Write a paragraph
similar to the one below for yourself right now, inserting your own
numbers. Our myth for Mary Ann will read:

*She came into this world to work on 3 (life lesson), with which
issues she has had serious difficulty in other lifetimes (missing number). She also wants to develop more fully in the double number lessons of 11/2 and 22/4 (life lessons). This entire life opportunity will
be filled with influences of the 9 Lesson (atmosphere lesson), urging*

*her to keep her path spiritual (if not "religious") in this lifetime.
Above everything else, her soul wants and needs to work on the
Lessons of 8(Destiny Number). If she will begin work on 1(success
lesson), the 8 Destiny work will be much more successful.*

At this point you may be impatient to jump ahead and look for
some "quick answers" to your life in the succeeding pages, but
please take the time to write out your new personal myth *in the
above manner*. While your conscious mind may think it is seeking
your personal truth, your unconscious mind is (right now) involved
in maintaining its old beliefs and behaviors. No matter how unhap-
py your life is at present, your ego has a stake in avoiding *meaningful change* by simplifying and toning-down the challenges in the
material you are going to read in the chapter "Numbers as Lessons."
It will seek only the glory words and will try to excuse or write off
the serious obstacles that are preventing happiness and spiritual
growth. If you did not have this self-defeating mechanism within
your unconscious mind, you would have gotten a handle on your
problems long ago. There are many kinds of "blindness."

If you are serious about self-transformation you must *see* how
your chosen lessons work together. A successful personal myth
must be integrated into your daily life. It must offer an explanation
for both the joys and sorrows you have already experienced in life.
You really don't want to begin this new journey haphazardly.

Once you have written out your myth, **then** (beginning with the
Destiny Lesson) turn to the appropriate corresponding chapter.
When finished, look at the Success Lesson, then the Life Lessons
(based on your birth name), and finally the Missing Numbers.
Afterward, look at the Atmosphere Lesson. Can you see how this
challenge is "following you" every day?

Now, rewrite your personal myth, including all the issues that
seem relevant to your life right now. If you find this procedure *does*
help you identify what you must do, you might consider (say, on
each upcoming birthday, as a present to yourself) rewriting this personal myth in the light of all the experiences of the year just passed.

*God utters me like a word containing a partial
thought of Himself. A word will never be able
to comprehend the voice that utters it. But if I
am true to the concept that God utters in me, I
shall be full of actuality and find Him everywhere in myself, and find myself nowhere. I
shall be lost in Him: that is, I shall find myself.
I shall be "saved"*

Thomas Merton, *New Seeds* of Contemplation

NUMBERS AS LESSONS

CHAPTER

One

There are two major dimensions to this number: The Creator, of whom there is but one, and your individual life, in and through which The One seeks to move. At The Beginning of evolution in space and time there was a ONE-ness to everything. And, mythically, all life is seeking to re-establish that Unity. There were no separated things; no separated heaven or earth at that time. There still is no real separation, but we are free to delude ourselves that one exists. The myths of many cultures and religions indicate a "rebellion" occurred in that Unity, with some of Its components becoming estranged.

The theme of this book is that The One is the Creative Force that we call "God," and we who dwell in the earth are the separated ones. The One has never stopped loving us and yearns for our return to Unity, but has left it to us whether or not we will return to His House; whether or not we will even be aware of this opportunity. Both He and we will be the better for this reconciliation when it finally takes place.

The following lessons are organized into "triads" or combinations of three lessons. Each grouping represents a dimension of growth we must all develop. The first of these is "me," relating to personal, inner growth. Then, "we," relating to interactions with others, and finally, "thee," representative of work relating to our relationship with The Creator. Lessons 1-3 comprise the first triad, 4-6, the second, and 7-9, the third.

Letters A, J and S have a value of ONE. The first concern with ONE is the above-mentioned restoration of Unity. Restoration is a process that proceeds individually, culturally, nationally and globally. This book is aimed at the work **you** as an individual can do, in your search for happiness, to create moments of this unity at first, if not a continual ONE-ness. The great psychiatrist, Carl G. Jung[1] said

> *I have frequently seen people become neurotic when they content themselves with inadequate or wrong answers to the questions of life. They seek position, marriage, reputation, outward success or money, and remain unhappy and neurotic even when they have attained what they were seeking.*

His diagnosis of the source of this unhappiness is our too-narrow spiritual horizons, and he prescribes that we seek to become "more spacious personalities." His goal for all humanity is "individuation," the fulfillment of our potential as a unique creature. Such "completion" requires intense self-study and continual effort, and the person must understand as much as possible about his/her own Light and Darkness. It is common to find ONES seeking power, reputation and, often, possessions, as evidence of personal worth and fitness for high status.

Over two thousand years ago Siddhartha Gautama (Buddha) likewise urged people to awaken from the tendency to live life "automatically," unmindful of their motivations and the deeds they produce. "Just go along to get along" was never one of his teachings. Lao Tze, the sage of Taoism in ancient China, a contemporary of Buddha, urged his students not to become swallowed up in the beliefs and values of a sick society, lest they themselves contract the illness of "normality."

One of the symbols chosen for ONE in this chapter is the circle, which has no beginning and no end, an ancient symbol for the Deity. Another ancient design, the *uruboros*, a snake eating his own tail, suggests "perpetuity" and the process of transformation; the UNITY of birth, life, death and rebirth.

---

[1] Jung, Carl G., (1963) <u>Memories, Dreams and Reflections</u>, New York: Vintage Books, P. 140

ONE calls you to discover your INDIVIDUALITY and to develop a willingness to know (and own) both the positive and the negative aspects of your personality. And also, your unique place in the universe. The individual working on ONE as a life lesson, Success Lesson or Destiny Lesson has the potential to become a LEADER, TEACHER, PIONEER, INNOVATOR OR INVENTOR, a WAY-SHOWER for others, or simply a ONE-OF-A-KIND PERSON. This means that you can walk in the footsteps of others only to a limited extent. To be sure, the need is to stand on the shoulders of one's predecessors, so that precious time and energy are not wasted in "reinventing the wheel." However, ONES need to heed their intuition and dreams, whether these come during sleep or through conscious, creative imagination. You can observe a strong CREATIVE urge in many ONES. BEGINNINGS is a key word with ONE.

Many born with this lesson begin quite early in life to show some "giftedness," or inclination to stand apart from their peers. As ONES grow in childhood they gradually become aware of their particular likes and dislikes, and give evidence of a unique temperament (not always a constructive one). Great tensions or conflicts can arise with peers or with parents who prize conformity over personal fulfillment. Learning to fulfill one's uniqueness while working within the norms of society has always been difficult for those who "march to the beat of a different drummer." Parents who have a child working on ONE should carefully monitor the child's education, making sure that apparent gifts are nurtured and expanded, but also ensuring a relatedness to society. ISOLATION can produce creative genius, but in a wilderness there is no one to share it with. Many gifted individuals lead miserable personal lives because they have so intently focused in just one area of life.

One difficulty for the talented person is a tendency to fall into ego inflation, which (s)he may try to maintain for a lifetime. The sinister side of ego can foster the illusion of self-sufficiency in such people, leading them to worship the little god of self. The danger for each of us, but especially the unique person, is egotism. It is a paradox that all of us must have a healthy ego to survive in society-as our armor. The problem with armor, though, is that its protective rigidity can cause us to identify too closely with our "outer person." We begin to think our armor is our true self, because we want and need its apparent strength so badly. Young people can go for years and years seeking to advance just the "false self" as Jung called it. Unless they learn to oil the armor of personality with the lubrication of the soul or Higher Self, it will grow more and more rusty, less and less capable of the versatility that Spirit requires.

Issues of IDENTITY can plague the ONE person. The self-centered individual can become increasingly self-obsessed and less able to do the soul work of EXEMPLAR or teacher for those who need inspiration. As time goes along the conformists in society will begin to ignore the innovator who has gotten "stuck," as a "Johnny One Note."

Each of us has a unique pedigree, fostered by thousands or hundreds of thousands of previous lifetimes in the earth (and perhaps beyond it). There is a justice and beauty to be discovered in each entity-we are all works in progress. Edgar Cayce said [2]

> *Each soul enters life to do that which no other soul*
> *in the universe could do as well...*

In the end, we must express our peerlessness if we are to be happy and find genuine fulfillment. When we think we have identified even a portion of our distinctiveness we are spiritually obliged to bring it to fruition in some overt activity. If our impulse contains flaws, we will be shown a better way.

Most ONES intuit the need for Something More Durable, a "unity connection," and often seek to fulfill it by giving ALLEGIANCE to Something Greater than the self, perhaps to a race, nationality, religious or political group, or sports team. Identification with something more all-encompassing than the self offers many rewards. Group membership offers the individual a safe environment in which to develop the specific abilities. Most

---

people nowadays probably need to begin their search for The Creator through such allegiances or identifications, and then transcend these for Something Larger Still.

The tightrope that ONES must walk requires maximum personal development without over-stepping into selfishness or egotism. Too close identification with the ego or personal self obscures what Jung termed "Self," or the highest experience that humans might have of God while in the flesh. The Creator needs our assent in re-visioning the essential ONE-ness of all that is. The ONE individual must not, however, expect to solve the world's ills all by him or herself. Creating and sustaining brief periods of unity in our lives is probably all the average person can expect, but we can treasure these as experiences of Something Bigger. I once heard a wise man say that, for the pilgrim, "peak experiences" are necessary, so that when we must traverse life's deep valleys, we have something exalted to look back on. Very few people are capable of seeing Unity in the chaos that seems to characterize human life. St. Paul said (Rom. 8:28):

> *We know that all things work for good for those who*
> *love God, who are called according to his purpose.*

If we acknowledge no Higher Power than our self, then the earth and its sensations are all we have-a god of turmoil.

If we accept Paul's words, the connection to eternity that many suppose is attainable only after death might be discovered now. The Creator is always here and now, in and around us. There is unity in any moment if we will seek it. Though we may not enjoy a particular life experience, we need to seek beneath appearances and evolve creative responses. The only other option appears to be staying in our "little god" ego consciousness, blind to the ways our ego defenses create so much of our suffering. As a ONE you need to take personal responsibility for the outcome of your life, to stand up for personal truths. The ONE person must accept a certain amount of aloneness in life if (s)he is to give a special gift to the world. Many gifted ONES permit aloneness to devolve into loneliness, and other ONES need to struggle with being different. Aloneness need not be loneliness.

You should see a strong desire for personal freedom and INITI-ATING activities in the individual working on ONE. This impulse can be exasperating for the parents or teachers who seek to guide that individualist. These guides will need a strong spiritual (though not necessarily religious) understanding as to what the individual's soul is trying to accomplish. Jung's term, INDIVIDUATION, was defined as[3]:

> *...an expression of that biological process-simple or complicated as the case may be-by which every living thing becomes what it was destined to become from the very beginning.*

By seeking to know the fullness of our individuality we discover a measure of The Father's Love in bringing us back into the earth at the present time. If we waste Life's opportunity in a search for conformity and seeking the approval of others, we deny our cosmic role in transforming the earth.

Number ONE, the initial lesson of this chapter, begins the first triad (lessons ONE through THREE) of personal growth and self- study. The three lessons relate to our identity and personality, the choices we make, and the work we do to become functional people. The focus in on us as individuals, and the inner world that we make for ourselves.

---

[3] Jung, Carl G., Collected Works 11, Princeton University Press, R.F.C. Hull, translator, "Forward to White's 'God and the Unconscious,'" para. 460.

CHAPTER

Two

This number indicates "ONE divided or split." The lessons here are CHOICES, DECISIONS, DISCRIMINATIONS, DIFFERENTI-ATIONS, OPPOSITIONS or SEPARATIONS. Jungian psychologists think babies (even at the embryo stage of human development) begin ego formation because of a perceived need for self-protection. As soon as ego formation begins, the child loses the sense of Oneness. Coping with this "differentiation" in the world of APPEARANCE is one of the TWO struggles.

The symbols chosen to illustrate this chapter are the parallel lines of separation or alienation, almost as if two armies are drawn up for battle against one another. In the second symbol these lines have engaged one another, perhaps in conflict or in seeking conciliation. Only in meeting together can conflicts be solved. TWO urges us to ponder our relationship with that which appears not to be "us."

The Creator has given humans free will to choose a path, if we must, that leads away from Unity. Hindu theology treats the observable world around us as "maya," or illusion. So, it may only *appear* that we can separate from one another and our Creator. One of my teachers says that all we are really free to do, in the end, is follow universal law and evolve our uniqueness. Maya leads us to believe we can operate outside cosmic law. One might expect to see both ONES and TWOS struggling with willfulness.

You may observe a tendency to ALIENATION in those working on this number. We alienate people when we physically, mentally, or spiritually eject them from our ego boundaries. This ejection is sustained by remaining concrete, defensive and rigid. TWOS who struggle with ALIENATIONS seem unable to focus on the whole person or object of "the other," just on some superficial aspect of them. We grow even more distant from others as we note more flaws emerging in them. In this way we create "enemies."

Our ego avoids understanding that the biggest defect lies in how we are accustomed to see the world around us. Fritz Perls[4] observed that as people become more and more ego-centered and concrete, they become less and less able to cope with their world, which permits them to function only when "in character." Ego maintenance then becomes everything in our life. The world of façade, mask or appearance becomes increasingly important to the individual who needs to look good. Great psychic and physical energy is devoted to the "correct" clothes, the "in" hairstyle, whatever it takes to "fit in." It is curious how "fitting in" with the "in group" is felt as expressing one's individuality. As the world of childhood dissolves, adolescents haven't yet developed adult securities, and those of us who have taught adolescents have surely noted the resultant "herd instinct." Both adolescents and adults permit their in-groups to dictate the acceptable forms of "independence" for membership–a real paradox.

Lives devoted to conformity prevent the wholeness that we all need to experience. In belonging there is only the illusion of wholeness, as non-members and alternate beliefs have been alienated. Perls noted that all groups and individuals form boundaries, and sooner or later this creates trouble with "the other," because we fixate on their differences and not on any community of shared interest. The TWO person can thus feel more secure in an in-group because of the illusive atmosphere of acceptability and "correctness." In effect they are only free within the confines of the in-group.

Franciscan Fr. Richard Rohr, founder of the Center for Action and Contemplation in Albuquerque, NM, is an exponent of "naming our illusions," and "knowing our sin," which might help TWOS to become more integrated. To Rohr, our personal talent or "gift" can also be our "sin" because we tend to use our gifts egotistically. So many times, as noted with the gifted individuals in Chapter 1, we over-use our strengths in competition or rivalry with "the other."

---
[4] Perls, Fritz (1969) Gestalt Therapy Verbatim, Moab, UT: Real People Press, p. 8.

Rohr espouses use of The Enneagram, a Sufi diagnostic device, to study where, how and why we tend to overdo. Our ego or personality needs to cling tenaciously to its personal illusions. Knowing this sin (definition: where we *fall short* of One-ness) and how we misuse our talent or power allows us to be more authentic individuals, less inclined to wear masks for others and ourselves.

Dr. Carl Jung noted that individuals who would not investigate their own "dark side" or "Shadow" of repressed material *must* project these traits onto others. The result is that we condemn our neighbor for unconsciously reminding us of negative tendencies that lie hidden in our own unconscious mind. It is probably healthy that we do repress certain anti-social urges, which can come to all people. But to fall into *condemnation* of others can truly be sinful, because it delays our own introspection. If their defect can create powerful emotions in us, then we are surely infected with the same shortcoming, and must recognize the fact. The ego, however, tends to avoid assessment of the miniscule kingdom in which it reigns.

If a TWO person struggles to live in the personality alone, he or she always needs to be right, because there are so many contradictions in this world. The TWO person then polarizes his/her views and lifestyle, completely shutting out other outlooks. Psychotherapist Fritz Kunkel said[5]:

> *The arbitrary preference for one of two equal opposites seems to be against [God's] will. If an individual deifies this kind of injustice, he worships an idol.*

Kunkel believed such rigidity to be the first step in personal decay: the more we seek to avoid something, the more we attract it into our lives. The TWO person would do well to become more versatile and more willing to live with paradoxes. Jung believed that "holding the tension of opposites" permits our creativity to emerge.

While some TWOS polarize their lives to just one "right way," you can also observe their opposites-those who prefer to sit on the fence and not commit to specific causes or ideologies. The issue still

---

[5] Kunkel, Fritz, (1943) <u>In Search of Maturity</u>, New York: Chas. Scribner's Sons, P.45.

is CHOICE but this second type prefers to keep all the options open. This type of TWO would do well to heed the truism, "If you don't stand for something you'll fall for *anything*!" This is probably the more common type of TWO, which can have no bottom line in belief or action. Both the indecisive type and the rigid type of TWO can demonstrate strange perceptions of truth. The former type can exhibit opportunism and a tendency to blow in the wind ideologically. Their understanding of what is moral is often purposely vague. They can jump onto whatever bandwagon of fad or trend is passing by, seeking deeper meaning in identifying with that which is always changing. Friendships, relationships and loyalty can thus be difficult for these people.

The very act of CHOOSING can be difficult because this individual can lack the ability to prioritize or discriminate between what is vital in life and what is not. I call this the "cable channel mentality." As one surfs the hundreds of channels on cable television, (s)he can find shopping services right next to religious programming; sports alongside documentaries on world famine, sophomoric comedy preceding a program on the world's great art or music, and each program has the same allotment of time and space. How do we formulate a scale of importance? By what standards do we CHOOSE? Is there a valid reason for any modern person to *have to* decide?

Without a base of values or priorities, all we need do is "change channels" when some element of a program threatens our egoistic comfort. All behaviors and events seem equally good for children thoughtlessly abandoned to the mass media, allowed to mature without some spiritual training during their impressionable years. Perhaps you will see in TWOS a tendency to "tune out." A wise teacher said, "Not to decide *is* to decide!" By our avoidance, we are moving ever closer to the future we'd rather not face.

Generally, the ego/persona prefers competition to cooperation; the opportunity to set oneself ahead of the others is enticing. There are many overt and subtle methods by which we can accomplish that. Those inclined to be active can engage in physical contests, where prowess becomes bullying. The more intellectual types can resort to weapons of sarcasm or verbal bullying. And those who are faint of heart can still engage in subterfuge, gossip or character assassination to topple the opponent. TWO leads us to understand the need for greater concern for others, and less for our own ego image.

There are many ego defenses that will delay or defeat such self-analysis. For that reason, the Christian Church established a confession system centuries ago, to allow the re-establishment of wholeness by openly admitting, and seeking to overcome, our dark tendencies. As western nations moved inexorably toward a culture centered on personal gratification, confession became not only less important, but is now scorned by many Christians. Great numbers of Americans now avoid self-scrutiny and, led by the media, are absorbed in voyeuristic judgment of the personal lives of entertainers or politicians. Such practices leave these viewers feeling self-righteous, but blind to their own shortcomings, doing nothing to bring healing to their own suffering hearts and minds. Fixated on the speck in others' eyes, they are oblivious to the timber lodged in their own eye.

There is an aspect to psychological projection, however, that can be very positive if the individual will work with it. We all admire others for a talent or gift they possess. I once heard a speaker say that every landscape we love is, in reality, the landscape of our own soul. Many individuals find it preferable to see another person as the gifted one or star, rather than take the risks of personal development. Many, many people in our spectator society feel that happiness has eluded them. They have not sought self-fulfillment–they have not become the star in their own life. It is more accurate to say that it is *they* who risk bypassing Life's opportunities. James Whittier noted in his poem Maud Muller:

> *For of all sad words of tongue or pen,*
> *The saddest are these: "It might have been!"*
> *Ah, well! For us all some sweet hope lies*
> *Deeply buried from human eyes;*
> *And, in the hereafter, angels may*
> *Roll the stone from its grave away!*

Why continue to live in a "grave?" It is not possible to project greatness on others if we don't already have some seed of their attribute latent within us! To begin self-healing we need to work at developing some aspect of the gift we admire most in others. We should not copy others, because we have our own creative personal "spin" to put on such abilities. As we will see in TWO's extension (FOUR) we must not compare our initial efforts at self-development to those of anyone else, especially the "mega-stars" in the field. Every world class athlete had to first learn to walk. Whatever we can develop now will be there for us to build on in our next incarnation. This is universal law.

In The Bible, Deuteronomy 30 outlines our obligation to come to a greater expression of unity, both within and without our person:

> *The commandment that I lay on you this day is not too difficult for you, it is not too remote. It is not in heaven, that you should say, "Who will go up to heaven for us to fetch it and tell it to us, so that we can keep it?" Nor is it beyond the sea, that you should say, "Who will cross the sea for us to fetch it and tell it to us, so that we can keep it?" It is a thing very near to you, upon your lips and in your heart ready to be kept.*

> *Today I offer you the choice of life and good, or death and evil. If you obey the commandments of the Lord your God which I give you this day, by loving the Lord your God, by conforming to his ways and by keeping his commandments, statutes, and laws, then you will live and increase, and the Lord your God will bless you in the land which you are entering to occupy.*

In the hope of these words, may you enter your "promised land" of individuation through the making of more spiritual CHOICES and DECISIONS.

CHAPTER

11/2

This is the first of the "master numbers" or "power numbers." It signifies the basic spiritual challenge. Look back on the computations you did to arrive at the final digit for each of your lesson numbers. If one of those sums was 11, you must state the final lesson number as "11/2," or 2 derived from 11. When a lesson number is derived from a double number, insert "spiritual" before the keyword of the single digit. In other words, you can have TWO as "choices," but derived from 11, the 11/2 lesson becomes "spiritual choices."

The individual working on 11/2 as a major lesson must struggle with all the earlier lessons of TWO, but must also face the profound challenges, which I call "The Christ Lesson." Though many holy men and women preceded him, The Master was apparently the first individual to face and overcome the world's illusions, including the great illusion of death. He said that His path was to be *our* path when we are ready to overcome this world.

If the visible world is The Great Illusion, represented by 11/2 it is the main obstacle to be overcome if we are to discover the goodness that God put here In The Beginning. The world's great illusion is that of SEPARATION, which is "the sin of the world." Any fool can *see* that people are different by skin color, sex, height, weight, and by mental and physical aptitude. Yes, any *fool* can do this. It takes the wise man or woman to transcend this visible separation, to find Oneness in humanity and honor it.

We have already noted that problems occur in human relationships because we unconsciously project our "darkness" on others. This activity happens automatically and unconsciously, so we must *consciously* mobilize the resources of our body, mind and spirit to overcome this natural tendency. It seems that the first step is to become *aware* of this inclination. The second step requires that we look inward and seek what causes our dark perception of "the other." It takes a dedicated person to do this continually, but it can and must be done. In 11/2 we may *note* the differences between ourselves and others, but we must refrain from *condemning* these differences. Compassion for "the other" is possible only when we lessen our own JUDGMENTALISM. If we would have compassion shown to us we must be prepared to give it to others. That is a universal law.

Ponder the great amount of suffering and sorrow that has occurred on this earth throughout history, because men and women could not see through maya (illusion) to discover the "brother or sister" in their neighbor. 11/2 is the lesson of BROTHERHOOD and SISTERHOOD. Granted, some individuals do not treat their blood brothers or sisters very well either, but 11/2 urges us to treat even the stranger as we would treat our blood relations on our best day. After all, can anyone who appears in our life truly be a stranger to us? Have we not already known them on some other shore, in some other realm, long ago?

Why *should* we be charitable to strangers, or those presented to us as "enemies?" The ego-centered individual cannot think of any good reason, I'm sure. Life, for egotists, is an ongoing struggle for self-advancement and self-defense, not sharing and caring. You will find many 11/2s involved (in the early years of life, when things seem so cut and dried) in condemnation of those who appear different. Many 11/2s must struggle with the illusion that *they* can become greater by diminishing some "other." Eventually this leads to a lonely, frustrated life unless they learn to correct the tendency, because everything and every one in this world is impotent and flawed in *some* way. Whatever imperfection we most strongly condemn, indicates our greatest fear for ourselves.

11/2 requires each person to face the illusion of an EASY WAY in the world–an opportunity to profit at someone else's expense. Look, for a moment, at the Tao symbol at the beginning of this chap-

...nt of these two segments as yourself and your ...one of these segments advance without loss ...ory? Would not that one lose something of ...f we steal from the present moment, we rob

...stice in life must understand that *equilibrium* ...al world. Only that which we have given can ...nt China there was an old proverb that said ...cut from one body will never stick to that of ...ve take wrongly from another person must ...that was destined for our future.

...iple "The Law of Returns" or "The Law of ...nd others call it "The Law of Karma." ...mply means "action," and the Law of Karma says we will receive only what we have generated.(See Appendix B) On the earth plane we need the illusion of "time," with its past, present and future, so we can understand the workings of this universal law. It is the principle of action and reaction, or of sowing and harvesting. It operates within our soul and is not imposed upon us by a vengeful God. Most westerners tend to associate this Law with eastern religions such as Hinduism or Buddhism, and are seldom aware that early Christian teachers such as Origen, Clement of Alexandria, St. Paul, and Jesus also taught it. In Galatians 6:7 Paul says

> *Make no mistake: God is not mocked, for a person*
> *will reap only what he sows.*

An excellent book on the many references to karma in the Christian scriptures is Dr. Herbert B. Puryear's, <u>Why Jesus Taught Reincarnation</u>.[6] Because of the illusion that a "quick score" is possible, many have been led into lives of crime and destruction over the centuries. 11/2 people must face every moral temptation that exists, and must strive consciously to overcome each. Many people throughout history have sought to eliminate an apparent "enemy" by

[6] New Paradigm Press, 1992, Scottsdale, AZ 85267

murder and genocide. In the Book of Revelation (13:10) in The Bible we read:

> *Hear, you who have ears to hear! Whoever is to be made prisoner, a prisoner he shall be. Whoever takes the sword to kill, by the sword he is bound to be killed.*

This spiritual law is inexorable. The only sure way to have something we do not have at present is to *work* for it. And one of the best ways to do such work is to supply others with those things (often intangible) which have not (apparently) been given to us (ex. love, caring, support, etc.).

Each 11/2 must face another facet of this lesson: striving not to make things more important in life than people and their needs. And that can be extremely difficult to do in a materialistic society unless and until one begins to "awaken."

"Choose you this day whom ye will serve...." (to what purpose you will direct your energies) is the admonition to The Chosen People in Joshua 24:15. There must be a conscious SPIRITUAL SELECTIVITY and it must be employed each day, or the illusory, shortsighted values of the material world will engulf you. This single principle is professed in all the world's great religions. Christians know it as THE GOLDEN RULE-Hindus and Buddhists as KARMA. Newton called it "The Law of Cause and Effect." The great precept here is our need of learning how to walk in our neighbor's shoes. I am certain that this is the major challenge of the Age of Aquarius, as our world is being called to a new consciousness of humanitarianism.

Two decades ago, a candidate won the presidency of the U.S. by asking voters to base their vote on whether or not they, as individuals, were better off in 1980 than they had been four years earlier. Voters were asked to make this decision from the self-ish point of view. There was no encouragement to look about one's neighborhood or city and decide if the mass of people, their neighbors, were better off. Echoing from Genesis (4:9) is Cain's question, "Am *I* my brother's keeper?"

Politicians should not be blamed, however, for catering to the nation's shared (if sometimes unspoken) values–politicians simply ride on the wave of "giving the people what they want." The quality of our government is no more or less than the result of the nation's unconscious values. *They* can't improve until *we* do. We *do* get the quality of government that the mass of people deserves. Most people are easily attracted to "something for nothing." The "graduation ceremony" for 11/2, if this lesson appears in your chart, is to want as much for "the other guy" as you want for yourself. In a society devoted to this principle we would not need to fear our neighbor. And we would have a "unity" that doesn't smother people.

11/2 is the struggle of the aeons between LIGHT and DARKNESS. Many suppose darkness to be evil, but the lack of light is rooted in ignorance. Or, even worse, in a lack of desire to even *want* to know the *full* truth of our life. Which one of us is wise enough to see *all* the outcomes of any event? Yet, our tendency is to categorize events as totally either "good" or "evil," without knowing the full implication or wholeness of the event. We usually evaluate such issues in the light of our ego or separated self.

The emblem of this chapter is the Tao, the ancient Chinese symbol of opposites (Yang and Yin) combined in the circle of One. In the symbology of 11/2 is found the struggle between SELF-ISH-NESS and SELF-LESS-NESS. If people fully understood The Truth they could not be selfish, but the maya of the earth plane blinds us, to the extent that we can feel justified living in politically or religiously-sanctioned prejudice.

Another issue that all 11/2 people must face is a weakness for becoming POLARIZED. It is understandable: most 11/2s understand their need to seek the Light and want to do good. Throughout history there is a repeated pattern of political and religious leaders (in order to bolster their programs, teachings or "truths," or to gain personal power) setting one group against another. People who have something to sell can more easily accomplish their goals by polarizing people and limiting their options by stacking the cards of available choices. It is also a device used in the entertainment industry.

Notice, if you will, how most of the violent films and television programs which attract us emotionally sanction their violence or depravity by shallowly portraying certain characters as "all bad." The viewer/participant (oblivious to other, more creative, options) is thus drawn to acquiesce to the scripted violence that ensues. It all seems justified and righteous to the "unawake" viewer. If you are an 11/2, do you carry this tendency over into daily life, letting others move you emotionally to do their bidding? In 11/2 there must be an equal amount of thinking to accompany your feeling.

As previously mentioned, there is much illusory comfort for "unawake" individuals in joining a popular organization. In-groups validate their members and offer some "meaning" (even though it can be one-sided and shallow) for their lives. Many times we, in our insecurities, need a group more than *it* needs us. In such organizations the leader with an agenda can manipulate followers by threatening withdrawal of group sanction or membership if the strict separations are violated. All such actions (ex. "shunning") violate the principle of ONE-ness that comprises the basic tenet of the world's monotheistic religions. Jesus of Nazareth taught that "a house divided against itself cannot stand." (Matthew 12: 25) A group or organization cannot survive happily by preaching oneness, yet failing to practice it.

Groups that separate us from our neighbor cater to our ego desire to be right, and remain a mini-god. Much darkness is fostered by the fundamentalist need for surety and apparent safety. When one is fixated on being correct some level of rigidity must follow, and one must separate from the brothers or sisters who will not similarly constrict or restrict themselves. The polarized person is not free to make up his or her own mind. Such individuals are usually unable to adapt smoothly to change.

If 11/2 is one of your lessons, do not permit others to use pejorative names that reduce your neighbor to a "thing." Beware of those who insert adjectives in front of others' names. Such code words can serve to short-circuit your thinking, leading you inevitably to the manipulator's conclusions. Any reference to your neighbor, other than "brother" or "sister," should be suspect. Educators know that listening is an active, rather than passive experience. If you cannot (or will not) listen to information sources and teachers with critical attentiveness, you become vulnerable to manipulation and control by others. And, if you allow only one human teacher to inform you, you are digging both your intellectual and spiritual grave. There are many "mansions" in The Father's house.

In Greek there are two words: *symbolos* and *diabolos*. It is easy to see that our word "symbol" originates in the former. Symbols usually bypass the conscious mind, reason and intellect, so that even the least educated viewer or listener can perceive some of their truth. Their deepest meanings are felt in our hearts and souls. Note the symbols used at the beginning of each new chapter. Each picture is worth a thousand words of explanation. The Master taught people in parable and metaphor because these communication devices speak directly to the unconscious mind. As such, symbols or parables prompt individual creativity and imagination, allowing us to find an "inner teacher." And this process often leads us to perceive a God who is far greater and more loving than He who is found in the printed or spoken word.

Diabolos, on the other hand, represents "that which separates" or breaks things apart, dis-unifying life. Here is the ego's desire to be "right" and to separate from certain thoughts, ideas or behaviors. Sadly, the desire for purity is so strong in some people that they engage in physical, mental, emotional and spiritual conduct that makes purity near impossible until they awaken to the Spirit's urgings. It is said that "the mind separates, but the heart unites." Until we blend heart with mind we will venture down many dead end streets. Many individuals conduct their lives from the intellect alone, condemning feelings or imagination as malefic.

On occasion, when I am lecturing, an individual in the audience will say earnestly, "But my religion told me I *can't believe* that!" when I propose an idea from the ancient wisdom. Such individuals are at a developmental stage where they require Truth to be served to them by others. At some time in early life we *all* must be in that nursery. But we can't *stay* in that dependency. Many just cannot believe there is an "inner teacher" which is quickened upon hearing a new dimension of "truth." The desire for "correctness" and pleasing "authority figures" causes them to deny the prompting of their heart, which wants to leap with joy when new understanding has appeared.

Some religious teachers operate strictly in the intellectual or analytical sphere, treating the written word rigidly–not validating their members' inner experience or personal interpretation. How much greater is the God that allows His children to be taught also from within! Is The Creator not everywhere?

Those who set the written word above (and in many cases dismissing) human experience appear to operate from the very energy (diable,diablo,devil) that they so strongly disdain. I have known many 11/2 individuals who strive mightily and sincerely to be "right," to know and do God's will. They are among my best teachers, as they model for me how hurtful to others can be the intellect that has not discovered the multitude of "gray areas" and is, as yet, incapable of mercy or compassion.

If 11/2 is one of your lessons, be happy. You have the opportunity to walk in the footsteps of avatars and masters, great people of Light. If you have allowed authority figures to be your only teachers, you will recognize precious few of the *living* saints who walk our earth. To accomplish the 11/2 soul mission you must will not to polarize yourself against "enemies." Yes, you *will* have to make many serious choices and decisions. You *will* have to get off the fence. You *will* need to examine your inner world (both Light and Darkness) and not repress it. What you do not know (or will not admit) *will* emerge and sabotage your life through projections and neuroses. You *must* certainly come to recognize which factors lead to greater unity or disunity in your life and the lives of others. You *must* struggle to avoid condemning others as you make your decisions, lest condemnation come to you.

11/2 symbolizes the soul reaching for TOLERATION of those who seem different, having been raised or educated differently. You have an obligation to consider all sides of a question or principle and not allow your insecurities to be manipulated by those with an agenda. There are many paradoxes in life, and you dishonor The Genius who made the universe if you seek only the easy answers or adopt only popular opinions.   If the Lord God had the infinite wisdom to design this world and others, can a soul operating with a robot or copycat consciousness ever find lasting peace in Him?

Finally, we must address the issues of revenge and retaliation. When the other has wounded us in some way, our ego structure usually demands some redress.   We take it upon our conscious self (which is so often asleep or without a clue to The Deeper Reality) to strike back at those who seem to have created our suffering. The person who can not or will not accept that KARMA is universal law will most likely create new difficulties for him or herself by taking matters of justice into his or her own hands. A major question here, one that you must ask yourself each day is "Can some person or event come into my life that I have not earned?" Is The All-Loving Father capricious? The temptation, when we are hurt, is to "fight fire with fire." Why then did The Master teach, "Do not set yourself against the man who wrongs you," and urge His followers to "turn the other cheek?"

Why did not Jesus, a most compassionate being, fight continuously against the evils of foreign domination and oppression, or rectify the many inequities and iniquities of His time? Why did He heal only those who asked Him? Why did He not use His heavenly powers to stay even the hands of His own executioners? Because His mission was to fulfill The Law. Many think this is the Law of Karma that he refers to. If you are struggling with 11/2, don't seek vengeance or retribution when you suffer at someone else's hands. Perhaps your soul chose the present difficulty in order to reconcile you to debts you incurred long before you became you. Or perhaps it chose to become a positive role model for others through the struggles you must endure.

It seems to me that The Master knew and understood this principle: that nothing comes to us that is not (in the end) GOOD. Even His own need to face the cross was good for those of us dwelling in darkness--a fulfillment from the time of "the first Adam." His message was to return good for evil, a most difficult challenge for all of us living in the world of maya.

CHAPTER

Three

This is the lesson of BALANCE or STABILITY. Using the symbol of the pyramid or triangle on the previous page, stop and think how difficult this geometric form would be to overturn. The third side of this figure gives a "return" or healing of sorts to the two lines that were going their own ways. If this is one of your lessons, find a nice pyramid photo and put it on your wall, where you can see it each day. It can inspire you.

A major understanding to be gained in THREE is that all of us operate in three dimensions: physical, mental/emotional, and spiritual. To have STABILITY in our lives we need to develop all three. The values that we hold spiritually must lead us to think and judge in a defined way, and those assessments lead us to certain physical actions or reactions. Many or most THREEs can see the need to work at two of these facets, but usually hope the third one will just go away. As a result, we get "pushed over" in life.

First, we are physical bodies. To keep healthy we must understand the requirements of our physical organism. Proper feeding is required, coupled with adequate exercise and care of the body. Secondly, we are mental and emotional creatures, and much of the activity of living takes place in our intellect and feelings. We are obliged to develop the mind as much as possible, and not let feelings betray common sense. The human capacity for thought and reflection raise us above the animal level. Neither should we ignore our feelings. They help us be human and need to be understood and honored. Many times our problems are first noticed in the feelings, and reflect some inner truth of which we may not be aware. Thinking and feeling must come into balance if we are to be happy and healthy. Thirdly, we are souls and we ignore this reality at our peril. Edgar Cayce, America's great spiritual teacher, often noted that we are not bodies that have a soul, but are instead souls which, for this period of opportunity, have a body. In THREE there is a need to recognize the strong inter-connection between body, mind and spirit. With most THREE people there are health or medical problems to be faced at some time in life.

In each of our three dimensions the issue of "diet" appears. For centuries it was understood that the quantity and quality of our food intake had a direct relationship upon our health. Some foods clearly promote good internal and external health–but not for everybody. There can be problems such as indigestion or allergies for some people. And some individuals are deficient in certain chemicals, and must supplement the normal diet with these as medicine. In other people the body can create an excess of certain substances. The health or BALANCE of the physical body is critical to all of us. Without equilibrium we cannot physically do our best work, and we may shortchange ourselves in accomplishing goals that the soul laid out before this incarnation.

It has only been in the last two centuries that medicine has taken seriously the influence of our mental "diet" on physical health. Most physicians today understand that how we think does affect how we feel physically. The dis-ease of stress, worry and anxiety in the mind and emotions can create disease in the physical body. Depression or unresolved grief can dramatically lower the blood's white blood cell count, creating a vulnerability to infection. This is a lesson that I learned the hard way some thirty years ago. The field of psychoneuro-immunology is a relatively new science that treats physical illness that arises from mental or emotional dis-ease. Fear and anger take a tremendous toll daily on people who harbor these two destructive energies. It is more and more understood today that anger hurts the angry person more than the target of their wrath.

Thirdly, we are spiritual creatures who have taken on physical bodies for a brief period in the world's history, in order to accomplish certain of goals in our return to Unity. We cannot ignore this eternal side of ourselves, but neither is it healthy to overdo it. We cannot claim to be dealing with any "reality" if we don't acknowledge our eternal side. To do the soul's work we must pay attention to our spiritual "diet." We are obliged to develop an informed conscience that can counteract the lies of the ego and the illusions in the world of appearance.

It is incumbent on us all to study the truths of the many world religions, in order to have a balanced understanding of Life around us, and to honor the paths that our brothers and sisters have chosen in returning to The Father. One great theologian said, "He who knows only one religion knows no religion." We are less likely to be misled by leaders if we can entertain the viewpoints of several faiths. As we study other religious systems we may awaken truths that we knew as members of those religions in other lifetimes.

We are obliged to nourish the soul's understanding, to give it breadth and avoid narrow mindedness. But we need a BALANCE here too. If we try to feed the body only on a single food we cannot be healthy. If we spend our lives totally focused on religious ideas or practices, we risk failing to ground our beliefs in the practicality of life's mundane tasks. Beliefs do not necessarily become faith unless they are confirmed through action. The best teachers of spiritual matters are those who practice what they preach.

Those of us who have chosen to work on THREE in this life can recognize that the dimension in which we de-stabilize most rapidly is, more often than not, the emotions. In our feelings lurk the villains of fear and memories of past hurts. In the emotions is a residue of soul memory from other lifetimes, both the attractions and repulsions. Our memories are constantly on guard lest those hurts come again. The endocrine glands of the body react strongly to emotions, most notably increasing adrenaline secretion as a response to apparent danger. In psychotherapy counselors can help clients avoid being overwhelmed by panic or fear by using cognitive therapies. In short, these treatments use what one knows to checkmate the deleterious effects of what one feels. Psychotherapy is a good example of a healing that can restore BALANCE.

HEALING is a major component of the THREE person's life,

either in giving it or receiving it from others–oftentimes both. In this healing a new meaning is often found in Life, as our soul continually seeks a re-connection to wholeness and The One.

People are complex and are thus usually unpredictable. Another attribute of THREES (until they learn better) is a propensity for "boundary problems." In early life many of us did not have an effective understanding of where self leaves off and the other begins. I am sure you know THREES who meddle in other peoples' affairs, inserting themselves into situations where they are not needed or wanted. For whatever reason (I think it often serves a defensive purpose in their lives, permitting them to put their spin on matters, or preventing others' threatening ideas from being heard) these individuals intrude on other peoples' privacy. They act inappropriately until they reach a rude awakening as to what is proper. This BALANCING is probably a process that all people go through in growing up.

It would seem that intrusion's opposite, APATHY, is likewise a THREE issue. Instead of over-connecting with others, the apathetic person fails to establish meaningful intellectual, social or spiritual links with the world around them. Many teenagers experience apathy when they have lost the certainties of their youth and have not yet formulated the truths of adulthood.

We THREES probably would prefer it otherwise, but we seem to learn best how to stabilize and balance our lives by facing IN-STA-BILITY and IM-BALANCES. As we try to cope with such difficulties, we begin to build defenses against being upset. As with the boundary problem person above, we have to integrate what we know, or what we have learned from experience into our feelings. Of course, some individuals are predominantly thinkers, rather than feelers. And these individuals need to insert more feeling input into their reasoning about life and its difficulties. *Learning* to feel sounds strange to many folks because feelings are a part of our makeup at birth. But for various reasons many people seek temporary shelter in denying their true feelings. Others pursue security by merely intellectualizing about life's experiences, as they fear the depth of their feelings.

The majority of people seem to live more in the affect or feelings, and thinking types must understand this feeling type. Good balance requires a mix of the rational and the non-rational in life. A pure rationalist will probably not purchase or read this book, as numerology really doesn't "make sense." Yet, as a non-rational technique, it can serve the purpose of helping people become aware of unnoticed aspects of themselves. Science, religion and medicine have a long history of using reason and logic in accomplishing their tasks too.

A great capacity to "feel" can help one individual be a standout, while a great excess of intellect over feeling can lead another individual to personal success. Exceptional individuals often abandon balance in order to make their unique contribution to society. Many of the world's great geniuses, composers, scientists or mathematicians, even many of the mystics, have been "unbalanced," and our world is probably better off for that. But each one paid or pays a high price for the instability in their personal life.

THREE often indicates your opportunity to turn dysfunction into functionality. Often you will discover a personal healing emerging from your suffering. Many THREES are VULNERABLE and must learn strategies for living with that susceptibility (whether it is physical, mental, emotional or spiritual) if they are to turn it to good use. You can find a necessity to integrate separated parts of yourself (perhaps some repressed memories) if you are to reach wholeness. Many THREES find a need to work with psychotherapists or counselors of some type, learning to build some depth into their lives.

The number THREE also symbolizes a HARMONY that can be sought inside or outside the person, or both. I have found that most THREES have an artistic side, whether in performance or in artistic appreciation. Most THREES have an enjoyment of music, and some enhance their workday with quiet or harmonious music playing in the background. There are a number of dancers that are THREES, individuals that continually strive for "balance" as they perform their art. The THREE person can enrich the lives of others if they seek greater emotional or creative BALANCE. Many have found a way of combining HARMONY and HEALING techniques as a personal gift. It often takes a sensitive person to do healing work with other sensitive individuals.

I have noted that THREE often turns up in the major lessons of individuals who rage or are overcome with anger. It is clear where the balance is needed here, but the cause of their inner conflagration may first need to be discovered. The angry person needs to diminish aggression while retaining a healthy assertiveness. Many males can have difficulty with anger that quickly becomes violent. I have also encountered women who have problems with "road rage" and others who control people in their lives through verbal or emotional tyranny.

Learning to INTEGRATE or to put all the pieces of our life together can be difficult. The integration process may require us to remember hurtful circumstances, so that we do not fall into them again. Pain is a great teacher if our ego is strong enough to permit it. If we cannot see the gift in our suffering, we integrate memories negatively, resulting in stronger fears about our the future. Children, especially, need all the help they can get in understanding their serious difficulties. If adults will not or cannot offer them this assistance, life will always seem threatening. Children will move into the future seeing the world as "contracting" rather than "expanding." Woe to adults who know only how to control children through fear!

THREE urges us to bind up our own wounds so we can convert past suffering into present day understanding. Many times a wound, when successfully healed, can cause the afflicted part of the body or mind to emerge stronger than it originally was. Sooner or later the imbalances of our past lifetimes must be faced and overcome.

THREE offers the chance to discover more about the wonders of the mind/body connection, and to discover new forms of self-healing. THREE's lessons conclude the first pyramid, or triad, of this numerology system, which relates to developing a balanced and stable personal self.

CHAPTER 5

Four

FOUR is the first of the "we" lessons that involve our relationship with those outside our self. The soul is seeking, in FOUR, to advance in the journey of "concern for others" that we began in TWO. If we apply ourselves, we are enabled to move into greater intimacy with people, which is a first step in our return to Oneness with The Creator. Lessons FOUR, FIVE and SIX, as the second triad, most strongly involve our human interactions. FOUR, as an extension of TWO might be seen as "choices involving others." If we cannot be honest with ourself we cannot be honest with others. Many FOURS begin life demonstrating strong traits of fantasy or wishfulness.

This is the lesson of HONESTY and SELF-DISCIPLINE. Note the square symbol at the beginning of this chapter. After World War Two, with the emergence of the baby boom generation, popular culture deemed it unfashionable to be "square." Old traditions that had provided stability (but also a stodginess, perhaps) to western cultures were now disdained by a growing number of the world's young, to be replaced by a "fun culture" that catered to the disposable income of the adolescent and immature. Old values, perhaps SELF-DISCIPLINE most strongly, came under attack in the expanding "if it feels good, do it!" culture. Many adults, perhaps envying the illusions of the carefree youth group, abandoned their shallow adherence to society's disciplines.

As the escapist drug culture expanded, self-restraint became unfashionable, and the young increasingly followed the Pied Piper of self-indulgence, whose message was that they need never mature, but could live indefinitely in escapism. Intemperance of all sorts was glorified in the age of "sex, drugs and rock and roll." Among the baby boom generation (which exists far beyond North American borders) it became popular to drop out of the old value system that society had evolved over thousands of years. Young adults who ignored those hard-won lessons slipped from refinement into lives of barbaric ignorance and self-indulgence.

As an extension of the Law of Cause and Effect, FOUR teaches us to deal HONESTLY with others, so that we don't reap DIS-HON-ESTY. In ancient Judaism the sacrificial altars were constructed in a square shape, and there is something sacrificial required in the FOUR lessons. Here, we begin to see our need to sacrifice some ego demands, so that our human interactions become harmonious. The post-war generation, reared in a time of unparalleled plenty has had to sacrifice little, because there has always been some way to get what they wanted. Credit cards, a seeming necessity during the post-Vietnam era, offered a way to live beyond our means. Many parents today find it hard to deny their children or grandchildren anything, and the concept of sacrifice seems absent from popular culture as a new millennium begins. As a FOUR person you may have difficulty with credit purchases or in saying "No" to your ani-mal self.

A major aspect of FOUR seems to be SELF-HONESTY and SELF-ACCEPTANCE. In this lesson we are required to say "Yes" to the gift of life that was given to us. There is an "Amen" or "So be it," quality to the self-discoveries we can make here. But we can only build for the future upon TRUTH. We shouldn't live in abject fatalism, without goals or hopes for something better, but neither should we expect some fantasy future where all ego desires will be gratified. Honesty with self moves us to accept both our individual light and darkness--the "givens" of our life. When we are willing to face both sides of our self, we build personal INTEGRITY. If we cannot or will not accept these, we build our lifestyle on lies. The soul's mind knows, and warns us, when we attempt to live a lie. You will observe many FOURS struggling with issues of TRUTH, both objectively and subjectively. In a world of illusion (maya), discerning the truth of people or situations can be very difficult for FOURS.

If we are to live TRUTHFUL lives, we need to accept every part of our past and see (perhaps with gritted teeth for a while) that only by passing through difficult experiences could we have come to the promise and opportunities available to us *right now*. Many people, when they have begun the process of personal healing (or faith building) look back and condemn the people and situations that seemed to hurt them. However, without those stimuli we would never have begun the transformation process. If FOUR is your lesson, don't condemn the people and events that helped you arrive at the present, which is always a *present* to you. You can begin healing or changing anything today if you are truly ready.

Projections keep us from seeing others objectively, and when our neighbors will not live according to the roles in which we wish to see them, we fall into anger, hate, discouragement or depression. FOURS, in early life, often fall for the other person's "mask" (some call it a "protective cloak") which says, "Here is how I want you to see me." Since masks and projections are meant to obscure the true person, we can only find unhappiness in such relationships if we accept their projection of themselves. For this reason FOURS MUST NOT COMPARE OURSELVES TO OTHERS. More often than not we compare our flawed self to another's false, projected image. We are not relating to their whole person, but only some small (and often untruthful) aspect of them. And such relationships are, sooner or later, doomed to disappointment.

When we compare ourselves to others we fail to accept the miracle of our own uniqueness. We also fail to see the bounty inside and outside us. Our Higher Self is not willing for this failure to occur, and regularly provides us with healing dreams and synchronistic experiences or déjà vu. These can be healing and elevating if we will heed them. When we make comparisons to others' lives we factor our own shortcomings and darkness into the equation. We see ourself as unacceptable and flawed and the other as just fine. How, then, can we ever see ourselves as worthy? In our perceived inferiority we will always berate ourselves, and fall into what I call "the four sins of FOUR."

These "sins," or shortfalls are (1) ENVY, (2) JEALOUSY, (3) RESENTMENT, and (4) SELF-PITY. They are forms of self-torture rooted in egotism, and are based in illusions. We never seem adequate in life because we are comparing our self to some mirage. And the sad part is that we waste precious time and energy (to say nothing about resources or money) in failing to ACCEPT our true self. If we are to grow to spiritual maturity we must build on the reality in our life. If FOUR is your lesson, work with the personal myth that your soul is now ready for self-inventory.

You cannot accept the truths of your own life when you live in envy of others. Your vision of "a competent person" will always be sought outside yourself. If you are unable to accept what is, you will be unable to accept what may yet be for you. If you cannot accept what is (or has been), you will live out this life as a victim, rather than as a shaper of your physical and social environment. Your relationships will always involve trying to change others, rather than risk change and new growth in yourself. Envy, jealousy and resentments hold us back from the opportunity of new growth.

We energize negativity in our life when we hold onto grief, self-pity and hostility–all conditions that isolate us from intimacy with others. We remain unable to fully commit our lives to new relationships, while we wait for some personal Godot to come and make us happy and validate our flawed ego image. Mentally or emotionally we will keep dropping out, "taking our marbles and going home," or else we'll remain stuck in love/hate relationships in life. Dr. Susan Jeffers[7] has written:

> We all know people who are out of touch with their pain–who have refused to let themselves feel their emotions. When we don't acknowledge our pain, it will be transferred to a bodily symptom, anger or something equally destructive. Saying yes means letting in the pain full force, knowing you will not only get to the other side of it, but also gain something in the end-if you look for it.

[7] Jeffers, Susan (1978) Feel the Fear and Do It Anyway, New York: Fawcett Columbine, p. 159.

We tend to compare ourselves to the very *best* individuals in certain activities. The ego then can say, "If I can't be the best, I won't play!" For many people, that attitude provides the excuse for failing to change and grow. But what if our present life's fulfillment lies somewhere in the *middle*, short of "world class," but satisfying nevertheless? In a society where being #2 or #3 is disdained, how can we ever find inner peace if we're not "# 1?" Note, for example, how professional sports' reporting glorifies only "the gold" of a single "winner."

Do you remember a 37th place finisher in the 1984 Olympics Women's Marathon event? Long after the medalists had finished, Swiss runner Gabriele Andersen-Scheiss struggled to the finish line, overcome with heat prostration. Crossing the line on hands and knees, barely able to move, she showed her personal greatness. As she completed the struggle to be *her own* best, who can say Gabriele did not embody all the courage and "heart" of *any* gold medal winner, and so "win" in this event? Today, however, the image-makers have reduced her feat to a mere footnote in Olympic annals. All over the world, each day and hour, ordinary people are "earning their gold" by meeting personal goals, being just one bit better today than they were yesterday. A society concerned with superficiality only wants to know the apparent "winner," and thus misses seeing the heroic struggles of the "losers."

FOUR calls us more to accept first who we *are*, than to fantasize about what we *might* be. In a materialistic society, so many that have found fame and fortune lead miserable personal lives because they have not yet found the courage to accept themselves. It shouldn't surprise you that in FOUR we begin to build character and courage, which reach a high point in SIX, as we need them in the relationship struggles found there.

FOUR teaches us that we must first know our *real* self if we are to be able to openly reveal ourselves in truth and love to others. You are likely to see a strong urge for SELF-STUDY in many FOURS as they approach mid-life. I know one woman, an adoptee, who spent considerable time, money and energy in seeking her birth mother in order to know her own personal truth.

Another aspect of this lesson is RESPONSIBILITY. Some FOURs will be seen as irresponsible in early life. Other FOURS can verge on compulsiveness in their handling of obligations. These latter individuals feel the burden of ACCOUNTABILITY, while the former ones need to find strength and determination to shoulder their apparent burdens. In FOUR we must show ourselves as DEPENDABLE through our stewardship of what <u>has</u> been given to us. Edgar Cayce taught that until we can achieve that acceptance and live by it, we cannot draw any greater amount to ourselves. TRUSTWORTHINESS and RELIABILITY are the qualities of the mature FOUR person.

Metaphorically, FOUR offers us the "cup of Reality" to drink or reject. At the fourth cup of wine in the Seder meal (the "Last Supper" for Christians) the rabbi from Nazareth ACCEPTED the final role given Him by The Father at The Beginning.

CHAPTER

22/4

Here, the intense work of spiritual SELF-STUDY, spiritual SELF-DISCIPLINE and spiritual HONESTY combine in the second lesson of "we." The 22/4 person must run the entire gauntlet of FOUR issues, including the overcoming of jealousy, envy, resentments, self-pity and personal fortune in life. He or she is faced with the challenge of overcoming SELF-INDULGENCE and/or LAZINESS. Usually the need to discipline self appears early in life. An illusion that many 22/4s must conquer is that of INFERIORITY or INEPTNESS, which can cause the individual to rely too heavily on others' opinions or approval. Such reliance weakens one's ability to individuate, and must be overcome. In addition, you are likely to notice many 22/4s striving to impress others and gain their approbation. Because projection (theirs and yours) is caused by, and leads to illusions, it is usually a wasted effort.

We might say that the strongest work to be done here is *SPIRITUAL ACCEPTANCE OF ALL PEOPLE AND EVENTS IN YOUR LIFE, BECAUSE YOUR SOUL HAS CHOSEN THESE FOR GROWTH.* One can expect to encounter many disagreeable people along this path. We have a need to see beyond these personalities and to discern what these experiences reveal to us about ourself and our own needs. Have you ever noticed that you gain more growth from difficult people and experiences than you do from pleasant ones? This lesson seems to instruct us that our best friends are the "enemies" that appear along The Path, and whose behaviors hurt us. The difficult experiences get our attention more quickly and show us what we don't want to continue in our life.

One wise teacher inspired by the roles we play in others' lives from lifetime to lifetime, observed, "Each person in our life has a purpose, even if it's only to show us a bad example!" We can learn from these "bad examples," whereas we usually don't learn much from our friends. Friends pretty much accept us as we are–warts and all, and seldom challenge us to investigate our life or make the big changes. But other individuals, disagreeable or even hateful ones, cause us to look into ourselves (if we are smart) to discover what we can do to avoid such hurts or difficulties in the future. They help us (often quickly) to overcome our inertia at effecting inner change. Such individuals or events can be so difficult that we never want to encounter them again, and we become willing to make major readjustments within ourselves. They can also sensitize us to a potential new role that we can play in improving society.

We can stop our growth in 22/4 at the "avoidance of pain" level, or we can explore the issue more fully, developing a more profound philosophy of life. In 22/4 we stand to gain a more thorough understanding of the basic issues underlying our difficulties. If we can learn from our suffering and maladjustments, we will develop a more truthful and sensitive conscience. New self-awareness permits us to change and grow into a new person, drop our old masks, and move more fully into the being that our soul has already forseen. There is a necessary process for shedding our false self, just as there must be an inner transformation in the discovery of our real self.

From earliest childhood each of us lives by a personal myth, or perhaps several conflicting myths. These offer explanations for who we are and why we do what we do, or why we avoid what we avoid. Though this flawed myth is a "hypothetical self," it is an identity that we soon adopt fully, believing this persona to be our real self. Most children take their myth of personal value from the experience of their treatment by others. Adapting to the authority figures in our life, we learn to do that which earns us love and approval from our elders and peers. We learn to avoid what is displeasing to them, usually sorting those "not me" qualities into our repressed self or Shadow. Because we need their love, *their* values become *our* values.

As Jung noted, we often consign potential strengths to the fearsome "not me file" in our unconscious mind, because someone else (whose love or approval we need in growing up) does not accept our thinking or behavior. Very few 21 year olds have fully worked out a secure self-understanding based on the truths in *their own* life. In adolescence and young adulthood's period of ego inflation, the tendency is to live a personal myth filled with hopes, fantasies, prejudices and many blind spots.

Only as life's experiences bring pain, showing us the emptiness in our adapted personality, do we begin to cast about for another, more durable "truth." Often, it is the actions or reactions of others (many times painful ones) that cause us to become more honest with ourselves-to build on what *is* in our life. There is often a struggle to ascertain just what "truth" is for 22/4s. Remember that the four double number lessons involve overcoming illusions of some type.

As a lesson, 22/4 requires us to learn to live from our psychological "center," doing what is "true" for us, and adhering less to beliefs and behaviors of those we have set up as experts. As is evident in the number of people caught up in trends and fads, and in "keeping up with the Jones's," the vast majority of adults are only partially liberated in this regard. Even in adulthood, our need for approval, love and acceptance from others is very strong. And many people would rather lead painful or ineffective lives of conformity than lose a relationship (even a painful one) with others. Perhaps the only way we can build the independence to pursue soul truth is through painful and disillusioning experiences. Then, we are set free to reorder *our* life and *its* truths. Expect to have many illusions shattered in this lesson.

The 22/4 person also learns to ACCEPT the consequences of his or her actions, and to avoid scapegoating others for personal failures. As American society enters the new century our nation seems ensnared in denial of personal responsibility when things go wrong.

We can achieve genuine growth only when we adopt President Harry Truman's dictum, "The buck stops here." I admire young Marines who are instructed to respond, "No excuse, Sir!" when their errors are challenged. One wonders how different history would have been if Adam had made this his initial response to The Lord (Genesis 3:12-13) or if Eve had spoken more honestly. HONESTY is the quickest route to personal growth and self-understanding. Only when we shoulder personal responsibility for outcomes in our life do we really take part in it.

When life's experiences trouble us, when people or events seem oppressive, our first impulse is to either struggle against them or flee them. This rejection tendency emerges automatically from our ego. In the 1930s and 1940s, during India's struggle for independence from Great Britain, many nationalists favored Mahatma Gandhi's non-violent civil disobedience method of overthrowing colonialism. But he told his followers that they could not arbitrarily break just *any* law they disliked. Drawing on the wisdom of Hindu scripture, he told them our first obligation was to try to obey the laws or conditions already in place. Only when they discovered these laws to be evil, were they permitted to break them. There must be a SPIRITUAL ACCEPTANCE OF WHAT IS before we rebel against "the system."

22/4, as a spiritual lesson, warns us that our soul (operating unconsciously) seeks out challenges and difficulties in order to find harmony and inner peace. But, remember that the ego seeks pleasure and self-gratification, and avoids as many challenges as it can, unless these trials offer illusive rewards of some kind. For each of us, real Life must be filled with difficulties, but not as punishment of some kind. The soul is drawn to lessons that will open our eyes and strengthen us in our transition into the role of "co-creator" with The One, The Lord and Giver of Life.

Only as we face the uphill struggles in life do we begin to gain authentic self-knowledge and personal truth. We cannot build endurance for climbing the mountain of truth by walking the plains of ease. The affluent world is becoming more and more the Pleasure Island of the Pinocchio story, a refuge filled with self-indulgence and the laziness of a "spectator life." If self-indulgence and playthings could have made us happy, they would have done so long ago.

Young adults, who see no alternative to living this life of lies, are experiencing more and more psychic pain because they have not yet discovered their spiritual needs. For this reason, many others claim life is boring. Often, their pain emerges from the unconscious mind in destructive and angry acts. The soul *knows* it has been sold a bill of goods by a society steeped in self-gratification as the highest good. Yet, spirituality that urges them to walk through the valley of the Shadow, can also repel them, as it threatens their wish for ego inflation. It should be no surprise that courage is born in the challenges of 22/4. The soul seeks the strength to swim upstream while other "fish" in society bask in the downstream current of conformity and materialism.

You will observe a need for order in many 4s or 22/4s. In some, this leads to obsessions or compulsions for neatness, orderliness or purity. Some of us facing this challenge compulsively encumber our lives with a host of rules and regulations in an effort to do the right thing. However, instead of fulfilling and moving us to individuation, over-organization imprisons us in rigidity. A rigid lifestyle thwarts the soul's desire to become versatile and responsive to Spirit. The search for a self-disciplined perfection can make us uncompromising and unyielding, denying us the prize of genuine freedom that we seek. I once heard a speaker estimate that over 80% of human suffering is self-inflicted, caused by our misuse of personal freedom.

Another quality, then, that seems indicated in this lesson is SIMPLICITY. It is easy to lose the focus of our personal struggle for meaning if we burden ourselves with attachments and obligations that do not serve our spiritual growth. Because of this, the monastic life offers a more liberating lifestyle than any modern student ever learns in school. In the effort to toe the line physically, mentally and/or spiritually, we saddle ourselves with rules and regulations which offer the illusion of success. Rather than freeing us, they increasingly inhibit our freedom to find solutions or answers in life. In the beginning of the SELF-DISCIPLINE process we do need some guidelines, but must not lose sight of the fact that these rules are but means to an end, and not the end itself. The mature 22/4 person can find him or herself seeking the essence of rules, restrictions or religious commandments, so that spiritual growth isn't stifled by non-essential minutiae.

Some 22/4s, in order to find their personal truth, may need to live very simple lives. In all the world religions we find those who have gone into a geographical or personal "wilderness" to more clearly hear the voice of Spirit. Western society has become afraid of silence or quiet periods, and continually fills such voids with noise and activity, which distract us from the normal process of reflecting on our lives.

22/4 leads us to ponder whether *any* person or event can come into our lives without a good reason. With The Master, we need to open our arms to *all* experiences that come uninvited into our lives. Wisdom dictates that we gain our nourishment from what is put on *our* plate rather than seeking some fantasy banquet that the other person seems to be enjoying, and which we would be unable to digest if it were given to us.

CHAPTER

Five

We are at the midpoint between the "beginnings" and "endings" of ONE and NINE. Critical forces are at play here. The desire of the conscious mind/ personality/ego to live in an illusion of control is very strong. The defensive need to CONTROL others and the environment around us must lessen in the FIVE experience. At the end of a cycle, inviting us, lies a re-integration of all life's experiences, and our eventual spiritual transformation. Resistance to CHANGE is strong in FIVES. The WILL is still powerful and OBEDIENCE to authority comes only with difficulty. You will see a "rebel" quality in many who struggle with FIVE. If we have difficulty in subordinating our will and behavior to earthly people, how much greater is our rebelliousness against God?

FIVE is said to be "the number of Man," and the five-pointed star (like the Chinese character *tai*, or "great") symbolizes the human being standing erect, head raised toward the greatness of Heaven, and arms spread wide in supplication. Relationship with The Divine is the keynote for the work to be done here. Those engaged in black magic turn the point downward, into the earth, as a denial of The Almighty.

The FIVE person is learning to accept CHANGE, especially if it comes at the bidding of another person or force outside the conscious self. That CHANGE is threatening to FIVES, we can observe in the RIGIDITY in which so many of us live. Sometimes we can observe COMPULSIONS or other FIXATIONS in such people. HOLDING ON to the people, possessions or sensations, even if these no longer supply happiness or gratification, is common. At other times you will spot OBSESSIONS (e.g. cleanliness, perfectionism or order) or DEPENDENCIES that this person must overcome. Eventually, most FIVES come to convince themselves that their compulsions are virtues. There is a paradox in many FIVES: they seek personal freedom but usually imprison themselves in some manner.

Early in life many or most FIVES came to believe that their world was not safe, and that they could not survive unless they became the designers and controllers of their personal wellbeing. They arranged and ordered their life in such a way that there could be no surprises or events that they did not choose. Unconsciously, such men and women learned to seek a single "right" way to live their lives–one guaranteed to avoid hurts. FIVE may be the developing soul's last refuge against Spirit, and all suffering or discomfort will be avoided if possible.

Even in those individuals who have found a temporarily workable system, you can still observe much RESTLESSNESS. Some FIVES come to believe that continual outer activity is the same as genuine inner CHANGE, but it only creates exhaustion. In the immature FIVE, you can observe a missionary zeal of projected certainty, which seeks personal validation by converting others to their own precepts or life style. Such a personality cannot endure gray areas in belief or behavior. They usually feel a need to hide behind the assurance of a dogma or doctrine. If their religious pose fails them, then their fearful core may stand exposed. If we can gain the adherence of others to our belief system, then it must be correct, right? Many FIVES prefer not to think too deeply about certain matters. If they make a loud enough din they can maintain their ego pose by being deaf to outside voices–even Spirit.

You may note a poorly developed sense of humor in some FIVES. RIGID people cannot allow themselves too much fun because the defensive life is so serious. The ego must remain ever vigilant so its fortress isn't subverted. Learning to laugh at oneself can be the start of learning to LET GO AND LET GOD. The author of The Book of Luke (21:19) wrote, "In PATIENCE [some say PERSEVERENCE] possess ye your souls." He was enumerating virtues that would sustain believers during times of trial. In taking the time to ponder the path we have already walked, we can begin to *see* some greater purpose than our comfort is being worked out.

As a new millennium dawns, as new trials and options appear for humanity, we might make this principle our watchword. Western society has come to expect instantaneous gratification in response to our smallest exertion. Without the inner discipline found in FOUR, it is hard for people to be patient nowadays. The accumulation of positive and negative experiences persuades seasoned adults to wait, watch and listen. Intemperate in youth, most of those who survive into middle age have to discover the need for "process" if they are to successfully reach their goals. St. Paul lists PATIENCE as one of the "fruits of the spirit" (Gal.5:22).

Trials and errors in early life allow elders to gain wisdom by reflecting on life's patterns, especially the relationship between cause and effect. In healthy traditional societies the elders' wisdom governs lifestyle. With experience comes the spiritual recognition that some force has accompanied us through life, often serving up what we did not want instead of gratifying our desires. Some years ago an anonymous author wrote "Paradoxes of Prayer," which illustrates this scenario:

> *I asked God for strength, that I might achieve. I was made weak, that I might learn humbly to obey.*
>
> *I asked for health, that I might do greater things. I was given infirmity, that I might do better things.*
>
> *I asked for riches, that I might be happy. I was given poverty, that I might be wise.*
>
> *I asked for power, that I might have the praise of men. I was given weakness, that I might feel the need of God.*
>
> *I asked for all things that I might enjoy life. I was given life, that I might enjoy all things.*
>
> *I got nothing that I asked for, but everything that I had hoped for. Almost despite myself, my unspoken prayers were answered.*
>
> *I am among all most richly blessed!*

If a FIVE person can hold to this consciousness, this FAITH, (s)he can live in EXPECTANCY that today's dark clouds won't be around forever-that something better is coming.

There is a strong ADDICTIVE urge in FIVE, which must be overcome if the individual is to find happiness. In some, addiction can be seen in alcoholism or substance abuse, but our world offers an increasing array of experiences or substances to which we can attach and addict. Power, gambling, sex, excitement, speed, overwork, and noise are some of the notable alternatives. Friends in the counseling field have told me that each addiction represents a soul search for the belonging or unity that awaits us in Heaven. But the addicted person, finding an experience that creates temporary feelings of connection or momentary exuberance, stops short of the ultimate goal and settles for a bogus paradise.

Deep attachment to addictive behaviors ensnares the individual in repetitive activity, long after the action ceases to give reward. What begins as a search for freedom or deeper personal experience now becomes an inescapable prison. Addicts lose the capacity for responding freely and creatively to new options in life.

You can expect to see FIVES living lives of DENIAL, as they refuse to face the true cause of their captivity. They will try to live almost totally in the ego or personality, unwilling to listen to conscience, dreams, or the promptings of Spirit. Rigid denial seems necessary so that the enslaved individual can maintain the fiction of living a life under personal control. Though their personal life is in ruins, the addict (or person of "patterned" thinking/behavior) will seek to avoid personal responsibility for the pain of life. If they are in bondage to alcohol or drugs it can be very difficult for others to convince them that they *do* have a serious problem. Slaves can find it hard to accept that they are owned. The need to escape addiction is often frustrated by those who love them...co-dependants. Many rigid or addicted individuals are propped up or supported by friends or family, who need to see the addict as "okay," so that they themselves can continue their own rigid behaviors. Misery loves company that it knows, and is comfortable with.

In an effort to banish doubt and uneasiness from your FIVE life, you may seek safety in REDUCTIONISM. This mental/emotional filtering process sees all new events and people narrowly, in the simplistic light of past experiences. People and procedures become categorized–"this is just another of *those* people or situations." You can find yourself thinking, "Here we go again, same old same old!" Recognition of patterns is a survival strategy; it's how we learn. But you miss seeing the true magic in your life if you pigeonhole people and events. Reductionism sees people and things as "only...." Yet, no matter how flawed we have become, our inheritance is to live as *companions* (not slaves) to The Creative Force.

There is a therapeutic process, The 12 Step Program, which offers a way to grow out of addiction. Transformation of denial into personal honesty begins when we can admit that *we* can no longer control our life, a confession that the ego fears most. Secondly, we must be willing to commit our life to a Higher Power (any being higher than the personality) or Purpose. This is an essentially spiritual (if not religious) act.

Curiously, these steps were the beginning of Buddha's Noble Eightfold Path, created almost 2,500 years ago. The Buddha's aim was to cure our addiction to desire and attachments, and ultimately break our chains to the earth and its pain, thus avoiding future incarnations. SURRENDER of our dishonest "masks" to The Truth of a Higher Power feels like extinction to the ego. The False Self of ego has been living as if it were a "little god," and must now give way to One Who Is Greater.

In Islam, the term "Muslim" is translated, "one who has surrendered to God." It is the surrender of our willfulness that blocks our experience of Heaven in and around us. The devout Muslim prayerfully stands with hands turned upward, open to Allah, then bows and kneels, placing the forehead on the earth, acknowledging The Lord's supremacy.

As we stand in our indecision, we who have become habituated to The Pit fear this: What if no one or nothing is *there* to take over once we have surrendered? Without FAITH, we are paralyzed by fear. It is not surprising that issues of TRUST and DISTRUST (both of God and our fellow human beings) are critical concerns for the person who has chosen to struggle with FIVE.

Patrick Miles Overton wonderfully stated the issue for we who need to make positive CHANGE, in his poem "Faith:"[8]

> *When we walk to the edge of all the light we have and take that step into the darkness of the unknown, we must believe that one of two things will happen–There will be something solid for us to stand on. Or, we will be taught to fly.*

Overton illuminates this predicament for the personality that fears to stand upon its own spirituality. The opportunity to move more fully into The Kingdom awaits us here, and it shouldn't be surprising that the ultimate goal of FIVE is FAITH.

We are most open to the ministrations of Spirit when we LISTEN and WAIT, both requirements of FIVE. When we can reflect on the path our personal life has taken, we have a chance to see that Another Force, a creative and loving energy to be sure, has always been with us. Then we may, as Cayce suggested, become aware that we <u>are</u> souls, temporarily gifted to live in a body. When we have surrendered our old RIGIDITY The Holy Spirit can teach us, enabling us to incorporate new, more versatile understandings of universal Truth.

Do you see why the acceptance of all people and situations (22/4) must precede victory over the FIVE lesson? Addicted people will do everything in their power to change the entire world around them, rather than initiate self-change, so their rigid dysfunction can be maintained. They learned early in life to MANIPULATE or CONTROL the people and situations around them in order to feel safe. Worshippers of some material idol, they never opened to the psychic or spiritual gifts that await them. In inner darkness, it appears easier to change the whole world than one's inner self. Controlling behaviors are a sign of the ego's dishonest defense against feeling personal shame. Addictive personalities, by limiting and controlling feelings, avoid the spontaneity that a happy life requires. Life, because Spirit continually draws us toward The One, *is* unpredictable.

---

[8] Overton, Patrick Miles, (1975) <u>The Leaning Tree,</u> St. Louis: Bethany Press.

Without FAITH we fear anything short of certainty.

The Qu'ran often links CONSTANCY with the need for PATIENCE. Buddhism teaches a patient "right effort," because it will evolve into an inspired consistency, and then into DEVOTION to a Higher Power. My strongest experience of Spirit at work among humbled humans has been in Twelve Step groups, where members have cast off the false self and slavery of ego pretense. When we arrive at a new, more realistic estimate of our spiritual self, FIVE offers us the opportunity to begin a journey out of the earth plane, which is our school, but has never been our true home.

In this look at numbers and growth we are headed, in the final triad, toward consciousness of The Kingdom of Heaven. Spirit operates continually in our lives, attempting to show us new dimensions in living, and we are obliged to keep our outlook fresh, willing to see the nuances in each new day. This process helps us gain FAITH by ADAPTING in the highest spirituality that we *know* to CHANGE as it occurs in and around us.

CHAPTER 8

Six

As the culminating lesson in the "we" triad, SIX leads us to learn about LOVE, which can only be learned by living in various RELATIONSHIPS with others. St. John tells us that "God is love" (1 John 4:8,16). If we are to shift our focus from the apparent "separated self" toward an eventual Unity, we must begin to acknowledge and relate to other creatures as part of The Whole. A person working on SIX should live daily with the myth that it is LOVE that brought our universe into being, and it is Love that sustains Creation each day.

Our need for LOVE, to give and receive it, is one of the most powerful urges that a human being can experience. Mother Teresa, when she addressed Western audiences, often said

> *The hunger for love is much more difficult to remove*
> *than the hunger for bread. If you judge people you*
> *have no time to love them.*

Another teacher has said, "When criticism comes in the door, love goes out!" As we seek to know more about God, we learn more about the nature of Love. As we learn about Love and nourish it, we grow in the capacity to want to know and serve The Creator. At any given day and moment we have the opportunity to join with that Cosmic Force and apply its energies in our lives. If we are to one day merge with The Creative Force, we must seize the opportunity to do so.

This chapter begins with the Star of David, a symbol even older than the Jewish kingdom of David. This six-pointed emblem was well known to the Egyptians, Indus Valley dwellers, Greeks, and The Chosen People of ancient Israel. Figure 1 below illustrates two individuals or forces approaching one another, as in the SEPARA-TION of TWO. Each has its own "balance," indicated by the stable pyramidal or triangular shape. In Figure 2 they touch or come into contact. Figure 3 illustrates a full embrace, pointing each one's energies outward and beyond this union. Inherent in this symbol is the suggestion that Love, as perfected in Figure 3, is a process, not just a single isolated event, as so much popular entertainment would have us believe. As a process, Love must move and expand and avoid becoming stagnant.

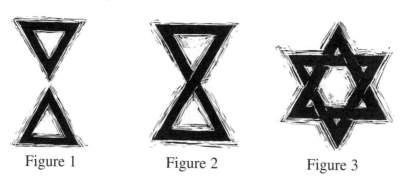

Figure 1   Figure 2   Figure 3

Figure 1 shows the attraction principle by which we become drawn to someone or some thing outside of us. Figure 2 suggests a meeting or touching of two forces or individuals; they meet and engage, drawn by some quality in "the other." In Figure 3 the individuals or elements merge, each drawn into deeper experience of "the other" by the mysterious force of Love. For a time there is the sensation of unity, of blending with all that is.

As we work from this love experience an inner transformation causes us to *want to* transmit love's energy to others. True LOVE is expansive. It doesn't limit, confine or restrict. It leads us outward from self to embrace others. Ideally, two balanced individuals can come together to do something greater than either can accomplish individually. Sexually, this can be apparent in the creation of new life–a child. And The Master, who embodied LOVE, proclaimed (Matthew 18:20):

For where two or three have met together in my name
[LOVE], I am there among them.

This means that if we willingly work in LOVE with others, not just mouthing the name of The Savior, we have an unseen help available to us, leading us toward Unity.

It is not merely for the development of Love that we come into physical life, or even for the enjoyment of it–mere giving and receiving of love is not the end. We are called to move from the idea to the acts of love and then to <u>becoming</u> love if we are to re-enter the consciousness of The Father's House. In our search for personal meaning we must recognize the necessity to *exemplify* all that we know of love. When we can totally immerse ourselves in that, we will understand the mystic Mother Julian of Norwich who wrote in <u>Revelations of Divine Love</u>:

He saith: 'I am the ground of thy beseeching.'
Wouldst thou learn thy Lord's meaning in this thing?
Learn it well;
Love was His meaning.
Who showed it thee? Love.
What showed He thee? Love.
* Wherefore? For love.*

The earliest humans apparently could not have feelings of love for a God they could not see. They created physical idols upon which to shower their devotion. Love must teach its primary lessons in our RELATIONSHIP struggles, with those we see and work with daily. The Master said as much. We need to love those in our imme-diate daily environment–a major challenge for the average person, as we attract those who mirror both our light and darkness. LOVE has the power to entice us away from self-concern, ego, mentality or persona, where we have sought refuge.

Love can, in fact, cause us to be oblivious for a time to our own self-interest and pain. It is not a passive activity. Love leads us to concentrate and focus on the beloved, and to desire a sharing of experience with them. And from this activity arises a combination of hope and faith in someone outside *us*. Erich Fromm[9] notes that FAITH and COURAGE must combine in the LOVE process:

> *To have faith requires courage, the ability to take a risk, the readiness even to accept pain and disappointment. Whoever insists on safety and security as primary conditions of life cannot have faith; whoever shuts himself off in a system of defense, where distance and possession are his means of security, makes himself a prisoner. To be loved, and to love, need courage, the courage to judge certain values as of ultimate concern-and to take the jump and stake everything on these values.*

In contemplating Fromm's "jump" we are reminded of Patrick Overton's "step out into the darkness." If SIX is one of your lessons, you should expect challenges to your courage from time to time. The word "courage" is derived from the Latin word *cor*, meaning heart-the bodily organ most often associated with LOVE, and also the distribution of life's energy through the blood. COURAGE requires mental and moral strength, and your SIX lesson may focus more on finding these than your dream lover. Most people, when they have walked the road of LOVE long enough, acknowledge the abundant struggle involved in this pursuit. You will find that you are incapable of sustaining lasting love relationships unless you strengthen your mind, morals and will. Notice that in figure 2 above, neither individual is supine and passive, sprawled flat on the ground. Both are involved and active, as they must be, if the relationship is to endure and prosper.

The process of building COURAGE based in faith (note that faith was a FIVE issue) requires you to confront FEAR. Committed loving relationships guarantee that we will have to face two types of FEAR: terrors for our self and dreads for our significant "other." Here, I think, if you have assimilated the spiritual work of 22/4, you

---

[9] Fromm, Erich, (1963) The Art of Loving, New York: Bantam Books, p. 106.

can fortify yourself with the acceptance that *nothing* can come into your life unless it is yours, and *must* be faced. Though your soul has chosen this struggle, your personality or conscious mind may seek to avoid it.

The people and experiences of this life opportunity are not there by fate or bad luck, or even as "punishment," but are way-stations and signposts on your return path to God. FEAR causes us to believe that we can lose the loved one, so we hold onto them even more tightly. The SIX lesson thus involves the avoidance of POS-SESSIVENESS of others. A wise teacher once said that true love is opening the sparrow's cage and saying, "Fly if you must."

Secondly, if your philosophy of life or belief system (this would include religious tenets) has been applied in life as you went along, you have learned to profit from what seemed to be mistakes. Armed with experience, you can better muster the courage to face personal fears and intimidation, because you have come to know that facing challenges has always made you stronger or more enlightened in some way. And there will be less fear for the loved one(s) when you honor all your life's experiences.

FEAR can paralyze us because it is rooted in self, and is thus the antithesis of LOVE. Many folks think that hate is the opposite of LOVE. But, to have the energy to fully hate a person, you must have had (or perhaps still do) love for them. One cannot just hate in a vacuum–there must be a background of perception or involvement with that person if hate's negativity is to be energized. Very often the hatred we experience for another person is an inner revulsion for our projected Shadow, which we see in "the other." Hate and LOVE are neighbors: the same coin–just different sides. Each one will link us in future lifetimes to those at whom we direct these energies. FEAR keeps us from loving–perhaps a too-strong concern over what will happen to *us* physically or socially if we fully pursue our love.

Genuine LOVE is willing to SACRIFICE, and even suffer, for the wellbeing of an entity outside our ego or personality. If we haven't learned (through the FOUR and FIVE lessons) to deny self, how can we find the strength to undergo the ego sacrifices that LOVE so often requires. If you do not evolve toward LOVE you will continue to live in the superficial and impotent "false self" lifestyle of the personality.

One of the greatest fears or phobias in America today is that of speaking in public. If you analyze the intimidation you will see that this terror is heightened by worry about how others see you, or what they might think about your efforts. As a teacher I have seen many timid individuals become dynamic speakers, if only momentarily, when carried away by a concern that allows them to transcend their ego. Imbued with a "cause" they became veritable tigers in communicating deep concerns in public meetings (e.g. city council or zoning board). It all depends on where your focus is placed. On yourself, there is fear. On the welfare of some "other," there is connection and you will forget to worry. When we transcend our separated ego self, all of us are capable of magnificent deeds.

We all know the stereotypical image of the mother who disregards personal safety and dashes into traffic to save her child. It is LOVE that, in the end, is stronger than FEAR. In the Christian scriptures we read[10]

> *There is no fear in love; but perfect love casteth out fear, because fear hath torment. He that feareth is not made perfect in love.*

As a higher dimension of THREE, SIX urges us to work upon our inner imbalances. In SIX, we are called to work with others in achieving new harmony, both as individuals and in relationships. In The Book of James (1:22) we are instructed to not merely intellectualize our love, "but be ye doers of the word, [LOVE] and not hearers only, deceiving your own selves." In street language, "walk what you talk!"

It is LOVE that permits us to forego personal advantage or possession, so that "the other" can find happiness. It is in SIX that GENEROSITY (CHARITY) is born, reaching its culmination, I think, in the struggles of EIGHT. When one truly LOVES, he or she wants to do something nice for "the other," who mirrors our uncon-

---

[10] The Boble, 1 John 4:18

scious side. We continuously encounter our total self in our relationships with others–our very best and our very worst. The ego and intellect always incline critically to see the defect in "the other," but the true spiritual disciple, working from the heart also, will commence self-study, improving his or her own personality. Under the Law of Attraction, we are then drawn us to even better companions.

Donald R. Peterson notes that his studies suggest[11]

> *If the affection of each person for the other is strong enough, if each person is secure enough to risk the creative explorations needed to find new ways of resolving differences, the ensuing developmental process may take the form of a dialectic, in which the action of one person is at first met by the contrary action of the other, but the actions, ideas, and emotions of both are continually replaced by a new synthesis. With open disclosure, each person reveals a part of himself or herself [that] the other had not known before. If the other accepts that and nourishes the special qualities of his or her partner, the effect can be one of continually enriched understanding and progressively deepening intimacy.*

From lessons ONE to FIVE our primary focus has been upon our inner self. SIX, as a multiple of both TWO and THREE, offers much to think on: choosing and balancing, now with people and events outside our self. Lessons SIX through NINE offer us the chance to transcend and enrich the limited personal self.

There is much indiscriminate use of the word "love" in western society. It might mean a preference or an attachment, lust, romance or mere sexual activity. Some people confuse over-sentimentality (because it makes them "feel good") with a genuine, sustaining LOVE. Youngsters growing up in Western society can become quite confused about LOVE's definition. Ancient Greek used "epithemia" to represent sexual lust, "eros" as love of the beautiful

---

[11] From Close Relationships, by Kelley et al., ©1983 by W.H. Freeman and Company. p. 391. Used with permission.

(as in two individuals drawn to beauty in one other), "philia" as the love friends feel for one another, and "agape" to mean "divine love." From my studies of literature and Scripture, it seems that the first three experiences are meant to lead us to the fourth. It seems to me that all LOVE is meant to instill beauty and harmony where little or none exists.

Perhaps the finest definition of LOVE is that found in St. Paul's First Letter to the Corinthians in the Christian Scriptures. In Chapter 12 of that work he lists some of the "gifts of the Spirit" that might earn a person acclaim within church or society. But then, in Chapter 13 he notes what any of these talents are worth if that person has no real love. Such an individual would be shallow and hollow, capable of noise but no real spiritual strength. Paul then lists behaviors that are holistic and in accord with the One Spirit: patience, love, lack of envy, boastfulness, conceit, rudeness and selfishness. The truly loving person is slow to take offense, doesn't keep score of others' wrongs, or gloat over the weakness and failings of others. Above all, writes Paul, true love is truthful in thought and behavior. The truly loving person can face anything, if possessed of faith and hope. These two are timeless, he says, but the greater, infinite energy is that of Love. This is why inspired individuals have called God "The Eternal."

CHAPTER

33/6

The individual whose soul has chosen this lesson needs to pursue the work very seriously. One who is not attentive to the "challenge quality" of 33/6 can easily go off the spiritual track. If this lesson was chosen by your soul, everything in the menu for SIX must be faced and spiritualized by you in the present lifetime. Lusts and loves of every type must be faced and raised to a higher level. If this is one of your chosen lessons, your soul is mythically attempting to manifest "agape (ah-gah'-pay) love." This is "God Love." Your goal is UNCONDITIONAL LOVE–a type of loving which says to "the other," "No matter what you do or don't do, I love you and will continue to love you." Elisabeth Kubler-Ross, who has written much on death and dying, has said[12]

> *The ultimate lesson all of us have to learn is uncon-*
> *ditional love, which includes not only others, but our-*
> *selves as well. Service and love are the only two*
> *things that are relevant at the end of your life.*

Take some time to look at the demands of 11/2 and 22/4. All of these illusions must be faced in this lesson too. Issues relating to self and self-ish-ness, of loneliness and isolation, and the search for One-ness with a Transcendent Force are here. Lessons of honesty, self-acceptance, bearing responsibility and exemplifying self-discipline are necessary. Difficulties with envy, jealousy, resentments and self-pity are sure to come into your path. Positive and negative projections must become conscious and overcome. It is hard to

[12] Kuebler-Ross, Elisabeth, Hospice lecture, Albany, NY 11/16/89.

visualize a person being successful in 33/6 work unless (s)he is *actively* seeking to know The Creator through some philosophy or religious pursuit.

The experiences that 33/6s must face can be maddening, and this person must remember that they are encountering the third of the "illusion" lessons that must be faced. If this is your challenge you must not become rigid in your thinking or actions. Much about The Creator's nature will come to you through difficult experiences and through intuition, where Spirit works best. You may endure periods of great doubt and/or distress during this life, and even have periods of agnosticism or atheism. Take heed of the attributes you may be projecting on God. Many agnostics, I believe, work on 33/6. At any given moment you can wonder where and how your own needs will ever get met. There are many demands on a 33/6, and you may approach the hour of death feeling that you have gained little growth.

When The Master died upon a cross, at age 33, His arms were open wide, accepting all of the physical world's experiences. He welcomed it all, even a humiliating death, if He were to awaken humanity to its inheritance. So must the 33/6 person welcome hardship and trials, as "the crown" is not easily won. Note how the FOUR, FIVE and SIX lessons combine here. Erich Fromm[13] wrote

> *The ability to love depends on one's capacity to emerge from narcissism and from the incestuous fixation to mother and clan; it depends on our capacity to grow, to develop a productive orientation in our relationship toward the world and ourselves. This process of emergence, of birth, of waking up, requires one quality as a necessary condition: faith.*

Although loving is an art, not all people are easily able to learn it or develop the faith in others that love requires. So much of our ability to love has been conditioned by previous lifetime experiences and the ways in which others modeled love for us during our

---

[13] Fromm, Erich, op. cit., p. 101

childhood. Without the help of an "awakening" most of us cannot move easily from underneath the shadow of our family tree. Remember it was our soul that chose the adults and family with whom we incarnated-those responsible for showing us either a strong or flawed image of LOVE. *We* selected them to help us "recall" where we had "left off" in our development in previous lifetimes. We all have been drawn to that which is needed in our present development.

As adults, until we learn better, we love others in the ways that *we* experienced affection in our formative years. C. Edward Crowther notes[14] that:

> *Children who learn the meaning of intimacy from their parents have scripts of love that will last throughout their lives.*

I once heard a speaker suggest that children automatically will project on The Heavenly Father the quality of their relationship (positive or negative) with the earthly father who raised them. A poor relationship with "the father image" may be a deficit to be overcome in early adulthood, before the person can give unselfish and unconditional love. And even if it cannot all be done in the present life, no effort is lost–as it serves as grace for a future life.

Struggling with issues of INTIMACY is a certainty for 33/6s. In our closest, most personal relationships we work out techniques for loving those we hold dearest. Issues of loyalty, privacy and confidences take on great importance. We must struggle to walk in our loved one's shoes, putting ourselves in *their* place, and pausing to consider the impact of our speech and actions before we do them. Some spoken words can be as lethal to LOVE as a hammer blow.

Here too, there is a higher dimension of BALANCE. While we seek to honor the loved one and his/her needs, we have to be mindful of our own needs. You can expect great challenges to your understanding of The Golden Rule, if 33/6 is your lesson. Several U.S. presidents in the second half of the 20th Century incarnated

---

[14] Crowther, C. Edward, (1986) <u>Strategies for Successful Relationships,</u> Santa Barbara, CA: Capra Press, pp. 20-21

with this challenge lesson in their personal lives while shouldering the burdens of office. If you care to work with the names of these ten men, spend some time pondering the difficulties in their personal lives.

The 33/6 person will feel as if (s)he has passed through a war zone by the time this life concludes. If one seeks entry to The Kingdom of Oneness it is necessary to confront the illusions that originally brought us separation in former lifetimes. We all must (in grace) walk our old paths again, this time prayerfully and consciously making restitution for our errors. 33/6 teaches us not to run from our VULNERABILITY, and is the true graduation exercise for souls who seek to regain Heaven. Until we accept our own vulnerability how can we muster the repentance necessary for reconciliation with God? Every issue in the 11/2 and 22/4 Lessons must now be faced and spiritualized. Much of our life on the spiritual path requires us to live at odds with the popular, yet false, values of Western society. It is impossible to progress in 33/6 while harboring the desire to be just like everybody else.

Another numerologist once told me that we have to *earn* the right to face the double-number lessons, and I believe this is correct. If one has not yet spiritually developed "the right stuff" for these challenges, this world's illusions will cause us to abandon the struggle to be more loving. You should not be surprised to see a goodly amount of chaos in the lives of 33/6s.

If you were born into a 33/6 name or birth date, assume that you *do* (at birth) possess the moxie to emerge more loving in the end, <u>if</u> you stay focused on the goal. At least once along the path of 33/6, I believe, you must experience a broken friendship or marriage. It is common to find 33/6s who have experienced betrayal of some sort. We can learn as much about LOVE by a split as by endurance. The worst situation here is to not learn anything from such difficulties. Not everyone learns best by apparent "successes." Some of us reap the greatest growth from analysis of our apparent "failures." In 33/6 every lesson in The Book of Love will be thrown at you.

One sure ingredient of this lesson is FORGIVENESS. You are certain to encounter individuals in your life who will grievously hurt you. The ego, always seeking its justification, will want to slither into the victim role and remain there, seeking comfort in blaming "the other." Such behavior (which seems automatic in most of us) overlooks that *we chose* this rendezvous with difficulty when we chose the particulars of this incarnation. We may have done so for purification of our old failings, or as a stimulus to new growth. It may be impossible to know which. In either case we cannot simply divorce ourselves from the problems that we chose for this sojourn.

Those seeking growth into happiness must genuinely forgive "the hurtful other" who has almost certainly acted with a "blindness" of some sort. The energy and inspiration to forgive others is most easily obtained by first facing *our own* broken-ness and need for forgiveness. If we remain locked in the personality or ego consciousness, our self-righteousness will blind us to our own imperfection and need for God's mercy. It is especially difficult to forgive the special people in our life who "should have known better" and hurt us anyway. Still, in the midst of our own pain, can we find the courage to help those others to heal and become better people?

The Chinese have a saying: "He who is bent on vengeance had best dig two graves." By retaining the sins of others and not forgiving their transgressions against us, we create a poison that begins to destroy us. Franciscan Murray Bodo, OFM, talked with the late Dr. Karl Menninger a few years before the doctor's death. Menninger was preparing a book on vengeance, and told Bodo that if a person's anxieties or problems are not genetic or induced by some trauma, such difficulties are usually the result of their inability to FORGIVE someone. Menninger said

> *The person cannot forgive God or the universe or fate, or their parents, for where they are in life. But most of all, they cannot forgive themselves [for being imperfect]. Therefore they subtly take vengeance upon themselves.*

Sufi teacher Atum O'Kane[16] urges those seeking inner peace to

---

[16] O'Kane, Atum, <u>Forgiveness–a meditation</u>, in Sufi publication The Messenger, c. 1987

accept, as the beginning of healing, and without judgment, that they *were* hurt by someone or something, and to recognize that experiencing hurt is part of the human condition. "The first part of you [that needs facing] is that place in one's being where there is the feeling of unworthiness or betrayal or a sense of guilt, the part in yourself that needs forgiveness without judgment." The person struggling with the 33/6 Lesson must first forgive him or herself for being weak and still imperfect.

Clinical psychologist Everett L. Worthington, Jr., at the University of Missouri, is director of the Templeton Forgiveness Research Campaign, and has been devoted to studying the positive and negative physiological side-effects of forgiving others since the 1980s. In an interview with Robert Owens Scott,[17] Worthington stated:

> *We know from research that when people feel less hostile, in a chronic way, they tend to have fewer cardiovascular problems, fewer heart attacks, and to feel less stress. They don't get or stay as agitated. The less stress a person chronically feels, the better his or her immune system functions. Many individuals who suffer through relationships tend to deny that they have been hurt and attempt to carry on with life, as if the injury never occurred. But until we bring these injuries to the surface, face them and forgive the transgressors, the injuries will fester within us and bring us dis-ease.*

Note that 33/6 is a higher dimension of the BALANCE and HEALTH issues of THREE. Dig no graves. Concentrate on *becoming* LOVE instead. If 33/6 is one of your lessons, and your RELATIONSHHIPS with others are in chaos, don't get too judgmental about your apparent "successes or failures." I find that a vast number of 33/6s, perhaps through their own struggles or the example they set, serve as unwitting teachers for those around them.

---

[17] Robert O. Scott's interview with Dr. Worthington, posted 2/1/99 at website www.spiritualityhealth.com

Unconsciously they seem to stimulate "the others" in their lives to ponder the true meaning of LOVE. For some, the 33/6 person serves as a good example, and for others, a negative one. 33/6 seems to cause individuals to function as a catalyst in helping others with the lessons of LOVE. In 1957 N. Sri Ram wrote[18]

> *Only as we go out in love which seeks to help and serve, do we transcend ourselves and develop that consciousness which embodies the awareness of our essential unity with others....*

St. Paul observed (1 Cor.13:13) that three things last forever: faith, hope and love. The greatest of the trio, he observed, is LOVE. In the 33/6 Lesson we are learning to live in love with the "otherness" that masks the unity possible upon our planet. Until we learn to love that which we *can* see on the physical plane, we will be unable to fully love, appreciate and understand That Which We Cannot See.

---

[18] N. Sri Ram, (1957) Thoughts for Aspirants, Compiled from Notes and writings of N. Sri Ram, Theosophical Publishing House, Adyar, Madras, India.

CHAPTER 10

Seven

The SEVEN lesson begins the triad of "thee," a higher realm relating to a more conscious and active relationship with The Creator. The issues, simply stated, are HUMILITY and SERVICE TO OTHERS, and they draw us into companionship with The Creative Forces in our inner and outer life.

When The Temple stood in Jerusalem (prior to the year 70), there was a great lighted candelabrum of pure gold in front of the building. It is the symbol for this chapter. Centuries before the temple was built, Moses had been shown the design, a candle stand with seven arms, and many students of metaphysics believe it symbolizes each person's potential for inner illumination. At first, The Chosen People needed an outer physical temple, to assist their understanding of an intimate meeting place between God and Man. However, it was meant to lead humankind to an understanding of our *inner* temple where worship must take place daily. The temple candelabrum represents the human body, and the seven lights may indicate the pattern by which Man discovers his capacity to walk hand-in-hand and co-create with The Father. The number SEVEN suggests a multitude of meanings, most of them sacred, and it appears over two hundred times in the Jewish scriptures alone.

Hinduism, over two thousand years ago, taught of seven energy centers (called "chakras" or wheels) within the human body--points of connection between the soul and the physical body. When the activities of these physical and spiritual centers are purified we can overcome most physical limitations and take on the role of "savior" for others. Sooner or later, each of us must give "such as we have" (Acts 3:6) to uplift our brothers and sisters in the human family. By accepting the disciplines of SEVEN we become better able to do so. If we are to reach the consciousness of ONE, we must transcend our personality self and act as if we are sons and daughters of The King, The One Power of the Universe

Those who are inspired to assist other human beings must be prepared to learn HUMILITY. Those who desire to lead others, and show them a better way, must first learn to follow. In the 1970s, when I began to lecture on metaphysical subjects, I had a dream involving an old elementary school. As I exited its front door, beneath a massive stone arch, I heard "the voice," which from time to time provides me with unerring guidance in my dreams: "Those who wish to teach must also be willing to learn!" it thundered. How true that has proven to be. One cannot do a numerology reading, give a lecture or write a book without turning inward and noting the "inner work" that remains to be done in self. And my over 35 years of teaching has taught me that it's never quite clear just who is the "teacher" and who is the "student" in any educational situation. It always works both ways. Many teachers are slow to discover this fact.

When Jesus of Nazareth overheard His students arguing which of them would have the highest place in Heaven, he told them,

> *Whosoever will be great among you, let him be your*
> *minister; and whosoever will be chief among you, let*
> *him be your servant. (Matt. 20:26-27)*

We must be prepared to follow orders before we can issue them to others. One must first learn to submit to The Power before (s)he can *be* a "power" in the lives of others. In the role of SERVANT we have the opportunity to shed our egocentrism and replace it with a centering on ONE. If we are to use our inner fire in a creative manner, our focus must include the needs of our apparently separated brothers and sisters. We cannot say we believe in The Creator, and yet hold ourselves apart from "children" that He loves as dearly as us. People working on SEVEN have a spiritual need to become involved in human affairs.

In SERVICE to others we have the opportunity and necessity to fully demonstrate what we believe about the nature of our God and His Heaven. In SIX we worked to more fully develop our LOVE, to bring us into closer vibration with The Creator. In SEVEN we must be prepared to live out what we have learned about LOVE. Most individuals drawn to work in the helping professions first need to learn self-care without, however, falling into selfishness. This process requires us to develop detachment, because we cannot help others out of their pit if we are in our own depressions. We may need to develop more dispassion without losing our compassion for those in need, and we will need to learn objectivity in relation to others and our role as their "helper." If we have personal shortcomings and failings, they will become readily apparent as we struggle to do our work. Nobody sets out to assist others without also taking on the task of restructuring *their own* personality.

Bernard of Clairvaux (1090-1153), founder of the Cistercian Order of monks, defined HUMILITY[19] as

> *...the virtue by which a man recognizes his own unworthiness because he really knows himself.*

Devotees of Dr. Carl Jung would immediately recognize Bernard's definition as an injunction to know one's "dark side" or Shadow. Bernard said:

> *For if you regard your neighbor's faults but do not observe your own, you are likely to be moved not to ruth but to wrath, not to condole but to condemn, not to restore in the spirit of meekness but to destroy in the spirit of anger.*

To be effective in SERVICE to others, most SEVENS need to more deeply understand other people; many are moved to become "amateur psychologists." One must make allowances for the vari-

[19] Evans, Gillian R. (1987) <u>Bernard of Clairvaux: Selected Works,</u> New York/Mahwah, Paulist Press, p. 103

ations in thinking, behavior and beliefs in the human family if (s)he is to be effective. There is no more frustrating work than SERVICE to others, especially to those who can not or will not see their need to be helped. And sometimes we learn that the best help is to refrain from helping.

Dr. Martin Luther King, Jr. said[20]

> *It really boils down to this: that all life is interrelat-*
> *ed. We are all caught in an inescapable network of*
> *mutuality, tied into a single garment of destiny.*
> *Whatever affects one directly affects all indirectly.*

Everything we hold dear relating to the Fatherhood of God and the Brotherhood of Man must be tested in daily application. The SERVICE you do may not be your main livelihood, but you can make it an avocation. Dr. Albert Schweitzer,[21] too soon forgotten by most Americans, observed:

> *...we must come out of ourselves, out of our voca-*
> *tions, out of our environments, and also be useful in*
> *human fashion somewhere and somehow. Everyone*
> *can find that. [We] must merely seek, wait, and*
> *begin small. Like the workers, whom, according to*
> *the parable of Jesus, the master sought for his vine-*
> *yard who stood around watching to see if anyone*
> *came to hire them. So seek quietly and modestly*
> *where God can use you and do not become tired in*
> *waiting and seeking. For if the word of Jesus-*
> *'Whoever seeks, will find'-is correct anywhere, it is*
> *here. You will discover where you can serve and*
> *experience the blessedness of this service.*

SERVICE is the low doorway through which we must all stoop to pass if we are to enter The King's Chamber. In helping just one person we take part in serving The One. And we further prepare

[20] King, Martin Luther, Jr., (1967) <u>Trumpet of Conscience,</u> New York, Harper & Row, p. 69
[21] Schweitzer, Albert, sermon preached in 1919.

our own self for Unity.

To the Hebrews there was a "fullness in the world of phenomena"[22] represented by SEVEN, often associated with "overcoming the earth plane." Consider here that those who seek might and glory instead of HUMBLE SERVICE, may just be prolonging their involvement in the limitations of the earth plane. The role of SERVANT seems to prepare us to rejoin the Creator, who wants us as His co-creators in the universe. Few modern parents urge their children into careers as servants. Today's preference is for money, power, position and self-sustenance, all of which can delay the soul's fullest expression.

An old Italian saying is that "at the end of the game the rook goes into the box alongside the king." And Lena, an old family friend, used to say, "Honey, there aren't any pockets in a shroud." Most of us know these truths, yet the majority of us still promote success in the material world as our children's greatest concern. In Walden, Henry David Thoreau said, "a man is rich in proportion to the number of things he can afford to let alone." The true SERVANT can help the victims of the wrong choice to focus on what is really important. Only what we build within is retained in eternity.

Ansari of Herat, the Sufi mystic, said[23]

> *If thou wouldst become a pilgrim on the path to love,*
> *the first condition is that thou become as humble as*
> *dust and ashes. Know that when thou learnst to lose*
> *thy self thou will reach the Beloved. There is no*
> *other secret to be revealed, and more than this is not*
> *known to me.:*

And Thomas Merton[24] urged

---

[22] Fillmore, Charles, (1931) Metaphysical Bible Dictionary, Unity Village, MO: Unity School of Christianity, p. 585.

[23] Singh, Sardar Sir Jogendra, (1939) The Persian Mystics: Invocations of alAnsari al Harawi, London: J. Murray

[24] Merton, Thomas, (1955) No Man is an Island, New York: Dell Publishing Co., p. 208

Do you want to know God? Then learn to under-
stand the weakness and imperfections of other men.
But how can you understand the weaknesses of oth-
ers unless you understand your own? And how can
you see the meaning of your own limitations until
you have received mercy from God, by which you
know yourself and Him? It is not sufficient to for-
give others: we must forgive them with humility and
compassion. If we forgive them without humility,
our forgiveness is a mockery: it presupposes that we
are better than they. Jesus descended into the abyss
of our degradation in order to forgive us after He
had, in a sense, become lower than us all. It is not
for us to forgive others from lofty thrones, as if we
were gods looking down on them from Heaven. We
must forgive them in the flames of their own Hell....

In SERVICE to others we will likely be moved to consider the
practicality in our understanding of love. If our love is more self-
ish than altruistic we are likely to find HUMILITY's companion,
HUMILIATION. If we have not learned wise personal boundaries
and give too much love to others, perhaps as co-dependents, we
will probably develop neurotic symptoms such as depression,
insomnia, or allergies.

The Book of Proverbs (16:18) says:

...pride goeth before destruction, and a haughty
spirit before a fall.

In SEVEN many of us are reducing the PRIDE that led us into
darkness in former lives. Some individuals come into the SER-
VICE professions with an almost messianic fervor that blinds them
to their own egotism. If we would be messiahs to others we must
work through the template of The Messiah, which the Book of
Malachi (3:2) calls the "refiner's fire." Malachi notes that such a
refinement and cleansing is necessary in order that we "may offer

unto The Lord an offering in righteousness." In SEVEN we must purge egotism, self-righteousness and pride from our personality if we wish to effectively serve The Lord and Giver of Life.

Most of us find the SERVANT role a difficult one to live out. There are not many "good servant" models outside the fields of religion and the healing professions. Because of the misunderstanding of separation between church and state, the good role models, inspired by religion, are not required study in public education. In colleges and universities, where true spiritual SERVANTS are often ridiculed, and where SERVICE is rarely a graduation requirement; degrees are earned for self and self's advancement. Over 2,000 years ago, Confucius said, "While you cannot serve men, how can you serve the gods?" For that reason, his philosophy was distinctly pragmatic and secular. He did not deny the spiritual world, but urged his students to live ethically first. Those in SERVICE to others soon come face to face with their *real* ethics, often needing to question just what they are doing and why.

The most adept SERVANT seems to need a foot in both the secular and the spiritual worlds. What passes for common sense in the secular world makes action its own reward, and seeks specific results as validation. If a certain activity does not seem to achieve our ego's need for results, we abandon the sometimes longer and apparently less-rewarding path that slowly leads to spiritual growth. The material world abhors the slow seasoning that takes place in dedicated SERVICE. Living primarily in ego and personality, the materialist fears to abandon the affectations of the ego structure. This tendency needs remediation in the work of EIGHT. Many times the SERVANT must deal with apparent failure as the end result of his/her action. The Master showed us this pattern in His apparent "disgraceful" death. We do not do our work alone, though, to the materialist, it seems so.

In 1970 Robert K. Greenleaf wrote The Servant as Leader, which shows how a person inspired by the vision and ethic of "the servant" can greatly affect the quality of society. It is his idea that the true leaders are the ones that are chosen by the followers. They are individuals who understand how things *really* get done. And they set a priority on serving others' greatest need.

The real power that so many leaders or managers covet arises from awareness, foresight and listening to underlings, traditional *yin* activities. The spiritual choice here may lie between personal fame and personal effectiveness in serving others' needs. Greenleaf later expanded these precepts in <u>The Institution As Servant</u>, which challenges traditional *yang* definitions of "power." The Robert K. Greenleaf Center for Servant-Leadership is in Indianapolis, Indiana.

In SEVEN we are learning to set self and self's goals aside, so that Something Greater may enter our lives. Experiences with HUMILIATION urge us to live less in the world of "me" and more in terms of "Thee." It is only when we sublimate our will to a Higher Will that we can most clearly hear the "inner voice" that prompts us to do God's work more fully. The Lord continually *seeks* our companionship and assistance in the ongoing evolution of Creation. As in Isaiah (6:8-9) we must be prepared to answer, "Here am I, send me." SEVEN invites us to our inheritance as "a part of The System."

CHAPTER 11

Eight

This is very much a lesson of applying our understanding of love, humility and service to whatever environment we find ourselves in. It denotes COMPROMISE and COOPERATION, both of which are difficult for those who cannot transcend self-interest. Many times, EIGHTS must work in situations where they are not the ultimate authority or leader. EIGHTS are usually drawn to institutions, organizations or groups in which they achieve a "middle management" position, and the stresses experienced there are a true test of one's capacities and beliefs. People "below" this individual can be extremely recalcitrant and uncooperative, and the EIGHT person must often struggle to gain their allegiance and collaboration.

On the other hand are the "higher ups" who can be demanding of the EIGHT caught in the no man's land where (s)he is neither leader nor follower. The promotions, pay raises and recognition, more often than not, go to the "big wigs" and not to the EIGHT person. And, many times, the ideas or compliance that our "middle manager" has elicited from the "followers" ends up attributed to the "leaders." Needless to say, FRUSTRATION is a constant companion in EIGHT's work.

Expect FRUSTRATION and a sense of LIMITATION here, occasioned by the illusion of "shortages" or "not enough." It is interesting to me that such a large number of North Americans lack the letters H, Q, and Z in the birth name, suggesting that there has not been adequate understanding in past lives of the plenty that pervades our universe. And how well are we learning the lesson? We have incarnated in a nation that is pounded daily by advertisers' messages of our limitations and personal inadequacy. Until we purchase this or that product, they intone, or forsake our individuality by adopting some fad, we can't measure up.

What is needed here is a certain DETACHMENT from the emotional need for personal achievement or worldly recognition. If EIGHT is one of your major lessons, this life is not about fame and rewards. It involves your motives and attitudes toward your work and the world around you. EIGHT represents the soul's attempt to work for the sake of virtue, downplaying the value of rewards. Cosmic forces both inside and outside of us have brought us to this happenstance as a test: are we willing (and not just grudgingly compliant) to set aside some ego needs in order that Something Bigger can take place in and through us?

Remember that this third triad of "thee" is more about moving into God's work than our personal achievement. Just as humility and service have drawn us to more transpersonal work, EIGHT now tests our readiness to work in The Kingdom as CHANNELS OF BLESSING to others. All over the world there are individuals praying to their God for some favor. And *you*, as an EIGHT, are invited into a new consciousness that *you* have the opportunity to serve as The Almighty's eyes, voices, hands and feet on the material plane.

As an EIGHT, why did you choose to incarnate in a society where greed seems to rule? Where best to develop the anti-toxin of DETACHMENT than here, amidst the contagion that your soul seeks to avoid? The economic system in Western societies is rooted in acquisition: that which can be seen and held in the hand (or in bank or stock accounts). The guardians of national wealth seldom pay even lip service to the unseen movement of Spirit in and through matter.

The EIGHT person can discover that matter is also holy, because The Lord made it all in the beginning, and saw it as "good." The key is: how do we *use* matter? As a person working on EIGHT you might read Matthew 7:9-11 and 10:29-31. The message of The Master (one that will never be taught in economics schools) is that each of us <u>already has</u> what we need right now to promote soul growth. It is the world of appearance that tricks us into restiveness. The amount of material resources allotted to us at *any* given time is more the result of grace than our personal striving. A God who is Love cannot and will not deprive His beloved children of any good thing. Our frustrations can diminish if we will learn that.

As an EIGHT you may need to study how many personal resources you are WASTING. The affluence of western civilization encourages waste on a grand scale, both in material and human resources. Food fights are a form of recreation among the young who have never faced famine or want. How many of us stoop to pick up a penny from the street? How much food and gas does your family waste each day? Yet we want "more." In a sense EIGHT is an "environmental number," relating to the people, places, events and things which are already present in our lives. CONSERVATION may be one of your major issues.

EIGHT is the number of the STEWARD who serves his Lord and Master–he does all he can with what he has. That effort to resourcefulness can stimulate the growth of a new talent. Any successful steward is a resourceful servant. This principle is found in the consciousness of Peter (Acts 3:6) who could only give the cripple man "such as I have." People of a new millennium must treasure the earth which has been given to them, if they are to recover consciousness of their divine identity. If we who are so often "asleep" cannot learn to sustain life on the physical planet that we *do* see, how can we be ready for a "heaven" that we *do not* yet see? EIGHT is about seeing heaven here and now.

Many EIGHTS believe they suffer shortages of time, space, finances, resources, support, material goods, and even the intangibles of love, affection, good will or friendship. There is a need to be mindful of the symbolism in the number EIGHT: an infinity symbol turned 90 degrees. It is by the spiritual use of our will and changed consciousness that we can accomplish this turning within ourselves. When we accept that our needs *are* met we can expand our GENEROSITY and channel more of our talents and resources to those who are needier than we. Coming to understand ourselves as NETWORKERS and CO-CREATORS with Father/Mother God, we move more completely into the destiny that has been ours since The Beginning. We become less grasping and envious. We overcome the other "sins of FOUR" (envy, resentment and self-pity) as we come to not just believe, but know that we are cared for (and *cared* for) by The One.

The plenty of The Kingdom is most beautifully illustrated in the story of Hanukkah–an event barely known or studied by Christians and Muslims. The story, found in the Talmud and 1 Maccabees (Chapters 3 and 4) of the Christian scriptures, bears retelling for those who have missed it, as *all* people should rejoice in its lessons:

The pagan Syrian Empire under Antiochus IV conquered Israel and polluted the House of The Lord, the Jerusalem temple, in 168 BC. To break the pride of Israel and its belief in one God the Syrians installed an altar to the Greek god Zeus in the place of worship. To Jews, the Temple was the building in which Yahweh, God, met annually with their high priest to reconcile them to Him. It was the place where atonement was generated. The foreigners profaned The House of The Lord.

Three years later a Jewish army led by Judah Maccabee liberated the city and holy mount, building a new altar and cleansing the temple for its rededication to Yahweh. However, relighting the temple lamp required more specially-prepared olive oil than was available; only one night's supply remained. The celebrants chose to light the sacred lamp, even if only for a single night. Miraculously the fire burned eight nights, until new oil could be sanctified for use. How great had been the worshippers' pain when their temple was desecrated. Yet, how much greater was their joy when The Lord demonstrated that He had not abandoned His people. Since that time it has been celebrated as The Festival of Lights on the 25th of the month of Kislev. I include the Hanukkah menorah at the beginning of the chapter, as a symbol of EIGHT ABUNDANCE. The illustration does not show the *shammus* candle from which the others receive fire on the eight nights of celebration, but what (or where) is "the fire" or "the light" from which all abundance comes?

Occasions of seeming shortage or deprivation offer us the opportunity to turn inward and integrate our knowledge and resources. Many EIGHTS don't use all their inner resources until they experience hardship. It is said that 8 is the "money number" among the Chinese, but it offers insight into *other* forms of "riches." To achieve that consciousness we need to COOPERATIVELY engage that which is already taking place around us.

Earth is part of the Heaven that was prepared for us. EIGHTS need to mix the "patience" of FIVE with the "balance" of THREE. Sr. Joan Chittister, OSB, writes[25]

> *Driven by a need for results, we miss the sight of trees growing and flowers opening and relationships becoming. We push and prod and commit ourselves to a kind of "progress" that misses a lot of life because we are not calm enough to let a thing develop through every necessary stage from slim beginning to satisfying end.*

On this plane of physicality and visibility we have the opportunity to discover (by trial and error) our true identities. In EIGHT we expand the PERSONAL RESPONSIBILITY that we learned in FOUR, and transform it into REVERENCE for all life. If we continue to permit ours to be a planet in dire distress, we dishonor The Father who placed it in our keeping.

The other symbol at the beginning of this chapter is the 8-spoked wheel used in Buddha's teachings. The sage explained that it is DESIRE, GREED or ATTACHMENTS that prompt our soul to continuously reincarnate upon the physical level, where suffering is a certainty. He offered his students "The Noble Eightfold Path" which, if followed for one or several incarnations, was sure to release them from the cycle of rebirth. The EIGHT spokes within the Wheel of Rebirth show this principle. Though proclaimed almost two and a half thousand years ago, these precepts harmonize well with the first two principles of the Twelve Step Program. First

---

[25] Chittister, Sr. Joan, The Monastic Way, Erie, PA: Benetvision.

is the acknowledgement that we have been unable to find happiness by ourself. Second, we recognize our need to live in a domain more spacious than our personality. Throughout this process, Siddhartha (who became Buddha or "awakened") urged his followers to be mindful of *what* they do and *why*, so that they do not sink into somnolent automatic behaviors in thinking or speech. This attentiveness is a key ingredient in Dr. Carl Jung's process of individuation.

DESIRE creates ATTACHMENTS that chain us to the object, sensation or person in future lifetimes. Make peace with your enemies now, while it is easy, so you don't have to do so later. Whether the urge is love or hate, it is sure to bring us back into a relationship with that issue or person in future lives. The ancient Persian sage, Zoroaster (Zarathustra)[26] chided his disciples:

> *Form no covetous desire, so that the demon of greediness may not deceive thee, and the treasure of the world may not be tasteless to thee.*

Zen Buddhists have as a principle that "Heaven is always under our feet," and the mystics of the monotheistic religions know this is true, as they have pierced the illusions of the material plane. When we are "up against the wall" with seeming deprivations or shortages, we can be inspired to find "a way out." We are then confronted with the need to muster courage to take a risk, and implement what have heretofore been only "ideas" or "hunches." EIGHT is a lesson that focuses on doing and applying, more than theorizing. Each of us has some "hidden genius" if we will venture to follow up our intuitions. The Kingdom of Heaven *is* here now, but it can remain invisible to those who embrace the material gods that blind our soul's vision.

Our willingness to put "a higher need" ahead of our *personal* gratification is the key activity here. Amid the circuses and sideshows of fearful planet Earth, the voice of The Ringmaster, The Cosmic Christ, still calls out to us, "Seek ye *first* the kingdom of heaven and its righteousness and all else *will* be given to you."

---

[26] *Wisdom of the Ages at Your Fingertips,"* MCR Software, 1995.

CHAPTER 12

44/8

One does not see this lesson as frequently as the others–it is comparatively rare and, when you see its challenging issues, you can understand why. As with the other double number lessons (master numbers or power numbers), in 44 we must face our illusions. The difficulties and trials are great, but so are the potential rewards. The 44/8 person must see through the illusions of frustration, rejection, limitation, and confinement that appear on the path. It might be well to read or re-read Bunyan's Pilgrim's Progress as the metaphor.

It is not likely that many 44/8 people will achieve what this world calls "success" any time in early life. There are so many experiences to be had, so many decisions to make, and a need to overcome the world's illusions before these individuals hit their "spiritual stride." All the illusions of 11, 22 and 33 must be met and struggled with on this journey.

Early life struggles frequently involve our capacity (or incapacity) to COMPROMISE with others. Many of the 44/8s that I have known are critical individuals who can quickly see the deficiencies in "the other." And it occurs to them, "Why *should* I make concessions from *my* high standards to accommodate this obviously inferior person?" Facing one's own power and pride issues is certainly involved in learning to reach adjustments with these "others." Likewise, in COOPERATION experiences, the 44/8 is certain to encounter obviously inept individuals, people so clumsy and ineffective that it is a wonder how they even got "in the game."

The spiritual disciple will be offered an opportunity to work with such individuals to "raise them up." And might 44/8 not be entertaining "angels unaware" (Heb.13:2) in this effort? Might not those bunglers be unconscious agents of a Higher Power, sent to strengthen the spirituality of the 44/8s, who so often come into positions of middle management or administration? There surely is a test of GOOD WILL here, as we deal with our (apparently) less able companions. Can you see why humility had to precede this effort?

An illusion for 44/8 is that earthly POWER is of any *heavenly* good. The 127th Psalm begins:

> *Unless the Lord builds the house,*
> *Its builders will have toiled in vain.*
> *Unless the Lord keeps watch over a city,*
> *In vain the watchman stands on guard.*
> *In vain you rise up early*
> *And go late to rest,*
> *Toiling for the bread you eat;*
> *He supplies the need of those he loves...*

Some are powerful in this world, and others are weak. In the end there is not much difference. Each is in his or her place because each needs to live the spiritual lessons of that role in the present life opportunity. As the psalm says, it is The Lord, The Creator, Love, which gives the increase to our efforts. The 44/8 person *needs to work* because work for a cause beyond self *is good in and of itself.* As we open our hearts and minds to a Higher Power we are nudged into the work we came to do. When we operate from the ego alone, we fall into bitterness at the "slings and arrows of outrageous fortune" that beset us in our quest for personal glory. The 44/8 is learning to put personal glory aside, so that a Greater Glory can be manifested in them.

Like the more highly evolved among the EIGHTS, this person must also experience the discovery that his/her needs *are* taken care of each day. They can then RELEASE egoistic striving for self, and begin conscious work in concert with Something Greater, even if they aren't quite sure of Its dimensions. As the false gods of fame

and fortune dissolve, our desire to serve increases, strengthened by
the assurance that each individual is capable of "leadership" in
what we do best. Find and read the old French story of "The
Juggler of Notre Dame," surely an 8 man.

If Heaven really *is* under our feet each day, as Zen teaches, then
it is impossible to depart from our soul's path. Whether The
Kingdom of Heaven is within us or among us makes little difference (see Luke 17:21). We can experience it if we but change our
outlook, thoughts and actions. The heaven we seek is not in some
far off place. Instead, it is to be found in a new personal consciousness, where we can frolic with JOY, serving ONE-ness
because we are assured of being loved and cared for—graced with
exactly what (or whom) we need each day. Here is "the garden" or
"the vineyard" of Scripture, if we would only see it. Many of us
are drawn to this secret garden, and I want to share a story about it
from one of my friends.

H (note his name starts with 8) was a well-educated man who
had fallen into the tyranny of alcohol addiction and had not been
able to escape it. One night he dreamed he walked past a magnificent garden, likely a square one (as the square can be a dream symbol for the soul and its integrity). Within the garden he could see
an old gardener at work. As H came to the garden gate he was suddenly outraged to find a whiskey bottle tossed by someone alongside the entrance. Fuming, he called out loudly to the gardener, to
complain that someone had littered what otherwise would have
been a perfect setting. Slowly the old gardener turned to face him,
and instantly H recognized that this old man was God. God, The
Gardener smiled at him and said, "Why H, *I* put that bottle out there
to draw you to Me!" The Old Gardener, The Ancient of Days first
placed His children into a garden (Eden) and has kept urging us to
see our world and its opportunities for what they *are*. A measure of
"Eden consciousness" is open to us all if 44/8 is our number.

The secular religion of Western culture has become avaricious
competition, while EIGHT and 44/8 draw us into COOPERATION
with a Divine Scheme. Competition has the virtue of encouraging
people to maximize their performance, and businesses *can* be

moved to serve clients with the best product for the least cost. Competition *can* lead to marvelous physical advances in society, but the spiritual world is different, as *it* draws us toward harmony and unity.

We cannot have competitors or enemies if we are to grow spiritually. In competitive societies too often, the end comes to justify the means, and citizens become ruthless and unmindful of "the least of these" in society. In competitive systems and organizations, too much emphasis can be placed on physical results, without attention to the means by which these are achieved. Spiritual or human issues end up subordinated to short-term gains. With a few exceptions, those of us who have incarnated in the Western world and were educated in public schools, have been imbued with ideals of competition.

Think back on your own education–how many opportunities were given to you for cooperation with your peers? And how many events were deliberately structured into team competitions? And what did those who couldn't "win" leave school with? In competition we work against the outer person rather than dealing with the heart and soul of this "neighbor." Cooperative experiences are much more likely to offer participants the opportunity to walk in their neighbor's shoes and find common interest with apparent "strangers." Cooperative ventures seem much more likely to stimulate friendships and self-esteem, as there doesn't need to be "winners" or "losers." And, of course, cooperative ventures allow something greater than "the sum of the parts" to emerge.

The 44/8 person must tend life's garden without concern over results as long as their motive is pure. It is typical of our materialistic cultures that we are fixated on quantity over quality, form over function, and appearance over substance. Yet, most of us are too mesmerized by the world's illusions to ascertain the workings of Spirit behind the scenes. "Looking good" has become the superficial standard in leisure-seeking developed countries, whether or not institutions or peoples' lives are decaying inside. Overcoming the world of appearance is a major task in the 44/8 Lesson.

Another major challenge in 44/8 involves understanding that

language can be used as much to obscure truth as to convey it. Most 44/8s have to learn that names or other labels may not lead us to any *real* understanding of a person, place or thing's true nature. Advertisers often select names or words to short-circuit our thinking, and appeal to our emotions. 44/8 urges us to peer into organizations, movements and individuals, to be more discerning of what lies beneath their image. We might otherwise find ourselves cooperating with un-spiritual forces whose goals we do not share. Things and images, mere "shadows on the wall" of Reality, must not be deified by EIGHTS. These are mirages that can quickly become idols in our life and, as our "gods," they must quickly perish. POPULARITY may be one of the most fragile of these "gods."

As with the EIGHT person, the 44/8 must struggle with ATTACHMENTS–those things, people, places or sensations that bind us to the physical world. We must eventually come to an understanding that our senses are able to perceive but a small part of what is real. If the masses of those who are "asleep" are forcing *your* gods to be the things and sensations of the earth, you will experience real pain in the withdrawal process to greater spirituality. As you seek to disengage from the apparent false values of society, you must not think that others will simply let you go. Those who stray too far beyond the shared values in their society or family are often "sent to the stake."

I urge you to get a copy of Plato's <u>Republic</u> and read Book VII, which is often referred to as "The Cave." If you have been a "follower" thus far in life, and have tried to keep peace in your life by just going along, this reading will make you uncomfortable. If you have tried to fit in by riding on the fads and trends of popular culture (which really haven't made you happy), reading these few pages of Plato will challenge your old assumptions about life. And when you have finished reading, reflect on the story: with whom did you identify most strongly? The instructor? The prisoners? The released prisoners? The individual dragged up into the sun? Or one of those who confers honors on the students? In the end *who* is *it*, really, that keeps souls prisoner on the earth plane? And what is *your* price of escape? A major illusion of the physical plane, which 44/8s must overcome, is that one has achieved something significant because he can name or measure things. These all must pass away into foolishness and insignificance.

There is an element of LIBERATION for those who struggle with apparent LIMITATION, as we come to see what is *really* blocking personal growth, both in the physical and the spiritual world. If we can willingly COOPERATE with others in an unselfish undertaking greater than our self, if we can willingly COMPROMISE with others, and will work for the welfare of the world around us, we can begin to see that the world *still* is good, as God made it in The Beginning. We can discover planet Earth is a place of ABUNDANCE, not of shortages. This realization may move us to seek a more honest distribution of the world's resources.

If we can DETACH from the illusions of this world, we can discover our capacity to take part in small "miracles" among earth's inhabitants. Without fear for personal sustenance or reputation, knowing that there will always be enough, we can release our panicky grasping at things and sensations. We can feel free to share who we are and what we have with others. The important thing, if you truly wish to do miracles, is to establish a mental vibration of GENEROSITY. Begin to give "such as you have" each day and each moment of that day. As you give, more is given to you–it is the universal law! Test it, but not with the hope of getting some *particular* thing back, as your payment often comes in some more needed or wonderful form.

When we no longer wish to hold back any personal ability or gift from The Creator, He makes us a more vital part of His work with humanity. On October 21, 1934 Edgar Cayce gave a psychic reading for a woman referred to as (681) in Washington, DC. He blessed her with these words:

The glory of the Father be manifested in thee as thou goest about to do the biddings that are prompted in thine consciousness. Dost thou keep His ways, His promises are sure, "Take not thought of the morrow"; for if ye abide in Him the word, the act, that which will be the blessing to thy neighbor will be given thee in thy work. WORK with thy hands, with thine heart, that ye may PRESENT an acceptable word that may quicken the heart of thy brethren; for he that saves a soul hath covered a multitude of errors. The FATHER abide with thee! The blessings of the Master, of those of old, of the knowledge of God that may be manifestly expressed in thee, be WITH thee!

Releasing our need to strive for worldly gain, we find the portal to a new dimension in Life. This process cannot be accomplished quickly, as daily determination and deliberate avoidance of the world's illusions will be required of you. And you will *always* be tempted to go "back to sleep." If you are working on 44/8 rejoice, because within your capacity for this lifetime, is the opportunity to become a conscious and active agent of The Almighty, filled with His grace and blessings for others. The 23rd Psalm notes that a table is prepared for us when we have passed through The Valley of The Shadow. It is the table of The Banquet to which we were invited before Creation. In EIGHT and 44/8 we find HOPE.

CHAPTER 13

Nine

Here is the omega number that completes the great cycle of ONE to NINE. It represents ENDINGS, and can be experienced in many ways. It is also the graduation lesson for the triad of THEE. When this is one of your numerological lessons, rejoice. You have reached an opportunity to complete a cycle of soul experience in this lifetime. In a sense this is the "death number" of a cycle, containing experiences of Scorpio, Pluto and Shiva energies.

What needs most to be remembered here is the soul's urge to TRANSFORM and RENEW itself. Life is a series of "little deaths" as we face and overcome the shortcomings of our past earthly sojourns. Each night, as we lay aside our consciousness in sleep, we die to the previous day's experiences. We need to sleep away from this world on a regular basis so that we can sort through our experiences and seek their value to our conscious life.

Violet Shelley[27] (1976) notes:

> *In Greek mythology the number Nine was consecrated to the 'music of the spheres' and to the muses, of which there were nine. The number nine played an important part in the life of the Romans. They celebrated a Feast of Purification for all male infants on the ninth day after birth. They buried their dead on the ninth day, and every ninth year they held a feast in memory of the dead. The Jews were enjoined to spend the ninth day of every month in fasting and repentance.*

[27] Shelley, Violet, (1965, 1976) <u>Symbols and the Self</u>, Virginia Beach, VA: A.R.E. Press, p. 17.

In NINE we become aware that something is culminating, because crises proliferate in our life struggle for inner peace and stability. The soul chooses a pattern of experiences before taking on a physical body at birth: "This is where and how I will attempt to rid myself of traits that are not eternally Life-giving." But the ego or conscious mind is seldom aware that this CLEANSING is underway. If there is no ongoing link between our ego and our Higher Self (Edward Edinger[28] calls it an "ego-Self axis") we interpret life's disruptions as undeserved or as "bad luck," or we scapegoat others. Many refer to such experiences as "bad karma," without realizing the cosmic principle of action is neutral-simply yielding a harvest that was sown in our previous activities. As noted earlier, the ego seldom seeks the fires of transformation unless it believes it can enhance itself during the process. If we practice regular dream study or meditation, warnings of our impending REORIENTATION will have been disclosed in advance. If we do not have a strong ego-Self axis, if we have been living solely in the personality, the need to change will seem forced on us.

If NINE is one of your major lessons and some "outrageous fortune" or "sea of troubles" is apparent in your life, I suggest you ponder the question: "Might this experience be one that *I* forced on some other soul in a previous life?" Edgar Cayce taught that we continually meet our self–who we are and who we were. You will miss the spiritual boat here, if all you can understand is "punishment." The ego, in its immaturity, says, "*I* would never have inflicted this pain on *myself*! It must be someone else that is doing it." In our tendency to project, we blame it all on God.

A God of Love *does not* punish people, but He *is* the author of a "tough love" that allows us to see the fruition of that which we have created with our free will. Such experiences move us, in time, to greater sensitivity as to where and how we are directing our energy. The Creator established The Law in The Beginning and permits us (as individual souls) to become our own teachers over time. In seeking to evade or avoid The Law we bring suffering on ourselves. In "sowing and reaping" comes the perfect justice that we all seek.

---

[28] Edinger, Edward, (1973) Ego and Archetype, Baltimore, MD: Penguin Books.

Many metaphysicians say that the main purpose of earth life is gaining experience. If we fully understood The Law of Returns, how many of us would continue trying to break Cosmic Law? What God seeks in us is "metanoia," the Greek word for "a transformed mind or conscience"–which we can achieve through REPENTANCE and REDIRECTION of our seeking and behavior. The NINE lesson leads us to a deeper search for personal meaning.

ATONEMENT is part of the menu of NINE. In one respect this word denotes a "making of amends," but another element involves a seeking for an at-ONE-ment with the Lord and Giver of Life. Our sufferings have the purpose of smoothing the rough edges of our comprehension. The sharp edges of the Alpha mature into the smoothness of the Omega. NINE involves a pruning of our past excesses, so that new growth is possible. Nothing can come into our experience that we have not invited with our past use of free will. I find that issues relating to violence must often be faced in the lessons of THREE, SIX and NINE.

Ideally, a NEW CONSCIOUSNESS will emerge from our sufferings and difficulties. When our flaws are refined in experience, all that remains in the crucible is the refined Unity which we had with the Creative Force in The Beginning. Edgar Cayce taught that we need not live continuously under The Law of Karma, but could move through our love and will into The Law of Grace.

Grace is the continuous outpouring of God's Love to those who seek His face and His ways, and it allows us to meet our "self of the past" less in "stings" and more in challenges. You may know the parable of The Prodigal Son in the Book of Luke (15:11-32). If you don't, look it up now. In it, we are told that The Lord does not merely wait for us to come to His door, but *rushes out* to meet those who turn homeward. Actively aligning ourselves with His Love diminishes our need to live under Karma. We must *will* to take part in our own PURIFICATION. The pain of attempting to live a lie will otherwise become your teacher.

In NINE we come to recognize our areas of darkness, and our need to be TRANSFORMED into People of The Light. Wherever there is Light, there is also Darkness, which helps define Light. But, wherever there is Death, new birth is also possible. The work to be done here is that of THE PHOENIX, that ancient mythological bird (birds can be symbols of the soul, which "flies" between earth and heaven) which had to die in the refiner's fire of PURIFICATION. From the ashes of seeming obliteration it arose to new life. NINE is the work of moving through the Valley of the Shadow of Death to RESUR-RECTION. No habit or belief can be resurrected until it has gone through a crisis or death. Unconsciously, our fear of personal death is stimulated when it becomes obvious that we must incinerate some facet of our old personality. And most of us will fearfully resist that seeming extinction. NINE teaches us that we can get *through* our time of sacrifice and emerge with greater integrity. One meaning of "sacrifice" is "to make holy."

The symbol chosen for this chapter is a bit abstract. In it you will find the three triads. But there is more there, and I will leave it to you to find your own symbolic meanings. NINE is something of a "mystery number" as it relates to forces that often are not comprehensible to our former consciousness. Chateaubriand said (in Attala), "Man must submit to the yoke without knowing the causes." Our misuse of our heavenly energy in past or present lives (the stimulus for our present condition) is normally unknowable to our conscious mind. And it is probably just as well, if we are to find the courage to grow. A link between the conscious mind and the unconscious must be built or strengthened in NINE. Dream study can be an invaluable asset to the individual seeking healing and wholeness, as each personal mystery needs interpretation and study. The Talmud teaches that a dream uninterpreted is like a letter unopened. Science has established that you dream *at least* four to five times each night. How much d-mail are you missing?

Wise therapists or counselors want to work with their client's dreams so as to understand the psychic energies at work. Dreams are our best friend, as they always truly, if symbolically, depict our inner condition, as well as a "next step" in our TRANSFORMATION *if* we will follow it. Their function is to illuminate features of our life that are still vague in our conscious mind. They contain not words (from which we can too quickly detach) but symbols (loaded with emotions from our "experience file") so we can gain the fullest understanding of our inner life. Meditation is another discipline that can lead us to our unfinished work.

Why is any PURIFICATION needed? Why not just make a New Year's resolution to "be good?" Why not just stumble and bumble our way through life, letting "meaning" appear in our experiences? It is a fashion among many young adults today to put themselves into hazardous spiritual situations, then wait "and see what happens." This pattern cleverly permits the ego to avoid personal responsibility for our life's outcomes. Such behaviors always leave us vulnerable to the ravaging of our animal self, the old, unreconstructed elements in our psyche—the illusory "easy way." Thus, we continue on under The Law of Karma, and growth becomes possible only through painful experience. The ancient wisdom sees us as pilgrims who have lost our way and are living a debased life in "a distant country." We need to arise and return to The House of The Father, to lovingly regain our full potential and work with Him in the ongoing work of Creation.

The NINE lesson is that of the prophet Jeremiah, who wrote (in Chapter 18 of his work):

> *These are the words which came to Jeremiah from the Lord: Go down at once to the potter's house, and there I will tell you what I have to say. So I went down to the potter's house and found him working at the wheel. Now and then a vessel he was making out of the clay would be spoilt in his hands, and then he would start again and mould it into another vessel to his liking. Then the word of the Lord came to me: Can I not deal with you, Israel, says the Lord, as the potter deals with his clay? You are clay in my hands like the clay in his, O house of Israel.*

The NINE experience encourages us to become clay that The Creator can reshape and reform, instead of our living in egoistic rigidity. Those in the deepest despair of this Phoenix Experience must understand that they are now walking through The Valley of The

Shadow of Death (Ps.23) and must not set up *residence* there. The "ashes" of the old self's destruction can become excellent fertilizer for our new growth.

At one of our conferences, Bill and I heard a woman say, "Oh, I understand NINE. I'm from Kansas, and these 9 experiences are like our prairie fires–they burn the old grass so that the new shoots of green growth can emerge." Willingness to permit new life in ourselves is most important here. Like Lot's wife (Genesis 19:15, 26) we often want to turn back to what is being left behind as a result of this REORI-ENTATION process. Twenty-five hundred years ago Lao Tze wrote:[29]

> *To be crooked is to be perfected; to be bent is to be straightened; to be lowly is to be filled; to be senile is to be renewed; to be diminished is to be able to receive; to be increased is to be deluded. Therefore the Holy Man embraces unity, and becomes the world's model.*

Those who have chosen the NINE lesson for this life experience have mythically chosen to have the old self "broken" through experiences, to yield and empty the old self, so that RENEWAL can take place. None of us can approach "being broken" with any relish, but we should understand that our *hearts* may, in this process, be *broken open* to greater love and mercy for suffering humanity.

When The Master celebrated Passover for the last time, He honored the thanks-giving aspects of the ceremony's past. He also pointed (in the ritual breaking of bread) to our need to be "broken" in our ego-centeredness for His (Love's) sake. Both the grain of wheat (the bread) and the grapes (the wine) must endure seeming destruction and re-formation in order to reach the table of the Seder or Last Supper. They symbolize the destruction of our "false self" which has grown in the earth, and this re-formation of our humanity is the Gospel Feast. This banquet awaits all who can dare to know *themselves* to be themselves, and yet ONE with God. The feast or banquet represents the Welcome Home Party for we who left Home long ago.

[29] Lao Tze, Tao-The-King, Sayings of Lao Tzu, Translated with commentary by C. Spurgeon Medhurst, 1975, Wheaton, IL, The Theosophical Pub. House, p. 64.

Making The Cycles Chart

Having studied the mythical challenges that your soul has set for itself, it may be worthwhile now to ponder a myth for the learning and experiences in your life thus far.

Edgar Cayce said that each letter of the birth name represents a "cycle of learning" chosen by *your* soul prior to birth. Nobody except *your* immortal soul has "imposed" your sorrows on you. I am presenting the work to be done in each of your cycles by offering a menu of challenges in the chapters of this book, each relating to a number's value. How might we work with Cayce's idea, forming a fairly accurate "learning chart?" In The Hidden Laws of Earth, by Juliet Brooke Ballard, (A.R.E. Press, 1979) the author suggests we use a typical length of life of seventy-five years, and divide it by the number of cycles that your soul has mythically chosen. The number of cycles equals the number of letters in the birth name. See why it's important to use the earliest name you know for yourself? The number of letters in that name seems crucial. I contend that we are always our birth name person, no matter whether we are later adopted, married or use a pseudonym. So, I have found it is safe to work with that first-known name, whether or not we still use it. I believe that we must use our middle name, if we were given one, but not necessarily a confirmation name, if your spiritual group uses one.

The resulting number from this division represents the length in years of each cycle's duration. After you have used my method, you might gain a more refined understanding of your earlier life by dividing the number of birth name letters into the current life expectancy for your sex (for those born in the U.S. this year, it is 73.6 for men, and 79.2 for women). Few people encountering a problem for a second or third time face it in the exact same way as previously. For instance, once you have done a 9 cycle you are likely to react to these stimuli in a more positive way, when faced with them again.

So, this process of looking at your upcoming cycles *can* offer you hope for better times in the years ahead, *if* you are willing to take an active and conscious part in self-transformation. Most important, I think (and we've had this validated time after time in our workshops), is that people can use this system to make spiritual peace with the traumata of earlier life, finally fitting the sorrows or sufferings into a comprehensive understanding.

Cayce's cycle concept does not guarantee that we will (or won't) live to age 75, only that if we're alive at a certain age, here is the work most in need of doing at that time. On our 75th birthday we apparently revert to the first lesson of our life (the M or 4 in Mary Ann's case) and continue on to our "end." Apparently the soul, when it can no longer make progress, or no longer wishes to, will find some way (perhaps an accident or illness) to conclude the life and move on. Let's see how this works in Mary Ann's case:

First, lay out the full birth name, leaving a generous space between letters, then insert the number values underneath, as you did in computing your life lessons:

M	A	R	Y	A	N	N	T	H	O	M	A	S
4	1	9	7	1	5	5	2	8	6	4	1	1

Then, use the table appropriate for the number of letters in your name in Appendix A. Insert the ages for the conclusion of each cycle into the chart. Mary Ann's dividend number, with 13 letters in the name, is 5.77 years. Her finished Cycles Chart will look like this:

Always start the chart with 0 to represent your birth. Note that I have skipped the ages of 34.6 and 69.2 in order to simplify the understanding of the chart. The 5 cycle after age 28.9 and the 1 cycle after age 63.5 are double in length, so there is a protracted experience of both the 5 issues and the 1 issues at those periods in Mary Ann's life.

Once this work is done, most people quickly look for their present age on the chart, and make some small mark in that space (perhaps a vertical arrow, which shows how much of the lesson work you have thus far experienced) to show "where I am now." If there is any value at all to this system of numerology, you must be able to recognize the conditions that you know you are experiencing right now. As you read the chapter on that number's lessons you should be gaining some insights on your current predicament(s) and see what Spirit may be asking of you during these experiences. Most people can endure difficult periods **if** they can have a myth about where it is all trending. And, of course, the <u>Great Myth</u> for us all is that of overcoming the world of pain and suffering.

If you have gotten this far, you have in front of you a new explanation for your life and what you have *really* been through up to this point. Remember, the ego continually wants to justify itself; it seeks to avoid responsibility for past failures. Ego wants to be blameless for the catastrophes you have experienced, and heartily dislikes seeing any redeeming value in them. As a creation of this plane of existence, your ego draws you to explain away the people and events that *your soul* has invited into this lifetime to help your transformation. Resist that. Look at this new myth with open eyes, so you can see the Great Work that is taking place in you, even on what appear to be "the worst days."

As you look through the struggles implied in the cycles you have lived through thus far in life, it might help if you made a list of your happiest and the unhappiest experiences so far. Next to each one place the date–as close as you can come. Without reference to specific experiences it can be very easy to make "cycle searching" just an academic exercise. At first, your ego defenses may not *want* to rehash the sorrows of injuries of the past. A truly vain person might not even want to revisit the fortunate events of the past, for fear (s)he has missed the "gift" that Spirit was offering. You must persist in your remembering because, without facing up to both what is perceived as "good" and "bad," you may miss seeing God's love, ever present in your life.

Now, turn to the chapter "Numbers As Cycles" and note some of the significant variations in a number's influence, depending on whether it is an overall lesson or a specific experience at a set time in your development.

Numbers As Cycles

1 cycles: As a cycle, 1 represents **NEW STARTS** or **BEGIN-NINGS**. In such periods there seems to be an optimum opportunity to begin new ventures, especially ones offering you further personal development. In a 1 cycle, I switched my teaching field from American History to Asian and African Culture Studies, a very significant move from the point of view of my spiritual search. Some individuals build or move to a new dwelling, some buy new cars, some take on a "new look," and some others marry or re-marry. In any 1 cycle the spotlight is on *you*, the individual. Thus, it is a time in which you can, and should, do something significant to enhance your capacity to serve more fully in The Kingdom. As already noted in Numbers As Lessons, **EGOTISM** is always a potential trap for one in mid-career, as perhaps it was for me.

Solitude may be a major feature of the 1 cycle experience. Aloneness can be a very productive adventure, and need not be negative. It allows us to turn inward and ponder our previous attitudes, paths or circumstances in life. Such contemplation, if honest, can also serve to deprive you of a temptation to scapegoat others if some project or plan does not work out. As the wit said, "Wherever you are, there YOU are." It is difficult to lose what you have made of yourself for very long.

1 cycles located near or after mid-life seem usually to be periods when the person is obliged to show the world just who *they* are. For many it is a time to lead, teach, instruct, innovate or move into a "pioneering" or "unique" stance. Remember that mythically, each of us has some "gift" to deliver to earth's peoples. Sharing one's talents or ideas with others, especially the young, helps the middle-ager to open up new potentials for learning within him or herself. Psychologist Erik Erickson calls this the "generative stage" of life. If we try to keep all our "goodies" to ourselves at this crucial time, we apparently create blockages to further personal growth .

You may find that a 1 cycle in your life will be a time to teach or practice "oneness," helping to bind up the wounds in groups or individuals, perhaps through some personal peace making or act of reconciliation. As we work to heal divisions in our world, we can bring people closer to The One, though that full realization can be hundreds or thousands (or millions) of years away.

As a first cycle, when the name begins with A,J or S, 1 seems to indicate a potentially gifted individual, but one whose early life can be dominated by poor self-image or low self-esteem. These latter concerns seem to need great attention in early life, as you build a stronger personality or ego base from which to offer your "gift." Some others have an ego problem right off the bat; some attempt to live a life of arrogance, where the self is placed ahead of anyone or anything else. As we used to say in the 1950s, this person is "cruisin' for a bruisin'." For the timid or indecisive individual there can be the need to **STAND UP** for some cause or ideal. Over the years in the classroom, I found many first cycle 1s to be "late bloomers," who rise to some prominence later than many of their peers. It should be noted here that whether one has a 1 in his/her name or not, it is not a requirement for leadership.

2 as a cycle: When a 2 cycle occurs you should expect to face **CHOICES** and **DECISIONS**. The easy decisions of childhood no longer seem available in adulthood. We can feel stymied by the "win/lose" qualities of our apparent dilemma in a 2 cycle. The "down side" of each selection can seem more powerful than any imagined reward. If we can remember the Hindu belief that "all life is illusion," we can usually move forward. Spiritually, it seems the only bad choice we can make is to make *no* choice. It seems easier for God to act on (and in and through) a "moving object" (one who has taken *some* decision, rather than none at all) than the individual who remains inert.

Another "choice" which is available at any age or cycle, but which seems more prevalent in a 2 cycle, is the manner in which we interact with our **NEIGHBOR**. Expect that you *will* be troubled by the words or actions of others in a 2 cycle. Will we treat "the other" as another of earth's resources to be pillaged, or as a venerable companion who offers us opportunities for growth on The Path? Will we seek to isolate that person or insulate our self from their life and problems? Will we succumb to the temptation to project our darkness on this person, and (if we do and are aware of it) will we then seek within ourselves for the "timber" lodged in our eye of self-righteousness? Or will we take the easy and ego-inflating course of condemning the person, their lifestyle, beliefs and/or actions? In any 2 cycle expect *diabolos*. And try to be on the side of *symbolos*. Emotionally immature people are more at home tearing things apart than joining them together in harmony.

As a first cycle of the name, the letter B, K, or T seems to indicate that great stress will be placed on the *quality of your choices*. Many times, as you must know, decisions can be made in terms of what is ego gratifying, rather than on what is truth or principle. People who have a first cycle 2 seem easily polarized in "black vs. white thinking" in the first part of life, until they begin to look inward and find some inner wisdom in self. Learning from the past seems a major obstacle to 2s. One teacher has said, "The definition of insanity is continuing to do the same old thing, and expecting something new to happen *this* time."

I have met some 2s who seem to need to learn to get out of their own way. Many of these individuals just do not *want* to accept the spiritual underpinnings of life, preferring the illusions of this material world as their gods. And, sooner or later, those gods *must* die. I have met a number of 2s who have made a lifestyle out of asking others for advice, but never following what is offered. As with the 2 Lesson, the issues of **PRINCIPLE, COMMITMENT, RELIABILITY** and **FOCUS** are important to a first cycle 2.

3 as a cycle: BODY, MIND, and/or **SPIRIT** are the arenas where 3 energies are most easily seen. As noted earlier, the soul is mythically working to strengthen its **BALANCE** or **STABILITY**. And, as noted earlier, we learn these two virtues by facing situations (inside or outside of us) of IM-balance or IN-stability. Expect something of a "rough ride" in a 3 cycle. Physical problems (disease) or mental problems (dis-ease, anxiety, stress) or spiritual problems (issues of faith or faithfulness) can assail us. All that is expected of us (as this is a learning period) is that we *apply* the knowledge we have. And perhaps we need to continue seeking further, and attempt to cope with the events challenging us. 3 cycles often can seem like a struggle that offers only "winning" or "losing."

As previously noted, it is in the **EMOTIONS** that most people destabilize the quickest. Most adults have well-developed "coping strategies" for dealing with emotional upheavals, and repression is a common one. "Just don't THINK about it!" is a common "cure." But psychologists know that "stuffing" genuine emotions can only lead to trouble later on. At one point in my younger life I thought I had found the perfect defense: Just don't let anything or anybody "*get* to me." "Stuff the irritation or humiliation, bury it, distract yourself with something else," I was convinced, "and the issue will just disappear!" But it won't; it all *has* to come out. In a 3 cycle look at your strategies for coping with upsets. Do they really resolve the issues that trouble you? Or do they threaten to bury it until a far less appropriate time. A therapist I know calls this "being ambushed."

As mentioned earlier, mental and emotional chaos *will*, sooner or later, create negative effects on your body's health. If you are in a 3 cycle, don't wait for something magic to occur in your life; *strive* to get some help with the difficulty. There are many physicians, counselors and advisors today, just waiting to help you. Thought is energy, which is a form of matter. Remember what you learned in science class: matter can neither be created nor destroyed. But you *can* transform it.

If you have **3 as your first learning cycle**, you must learn not to react to life's problems in a primarily *emotional* way. If you are a sensitive person, use the sensitivity in some constructive artistic or musical way. I have known a great number of 3s who just cannot muster much logic or reasoning in the face of crises. They tend to over-react. It is as if they believe that being immediately forceful against the person or idea can "bury" the adversary in words or violence. They become more victims than victors along The Path because some of them have family, friends or peers who long ago learned how to manipulate them. Their emotional "buttons" have become so obvious. The wisdom of the Tao urges us to make our life equal parts of feeling and thinking.

The 4 cycle: This is a time to practice **HONESTY** with others and with yourself. Most people are concerned about the quality of their relationships, and such quality begins *here*, in the need for HONESTY *first* with self. We must remain conscious of the mind games (e.g. denial, projection, scapegoating) which are easy to fall into. Issues of **RESPONSIBILITY** can seem overwhelming in 4 cycles. We must be mindful of the ways in which we avoid **TRUTH** in our lives with shallow ego defenses. If we lie to ourselves we are sure to lie to others. A mental and emotional **SELF-DISCIPLNE** must be practiced in a 4 cycle above all other cycles. If we are to go forward in wholeness we must remember our tendency to lapse into destructive patterns of our past. More than in other cycles, the 4 seems to want to lure us back into periods of **ENVY, JEALOUSY, RESENTMENTS** and **SELF-PITY**. Emotional insecurities can plague us, and we can strongly desire to be liked and like everyone else, which may have been part of our problem from the beginning.

In any 4 cycle, but especially **if your name begins with D, M or V**, you must resolve to operate from your "center," that storehouse of memories of what *is* good for the spiritual self and what is *not*. You should expect to be tempted to "people pleasing" speech or actions in a 4 cycle.

People whose names begin with a 4 cycle seem to have arrived in the present life feeling inferior or inept in some way. Early on, children can fall into the pattern of copying *someone else's* "success path," as if that can guarantee safety or survival. Physical survival, perhaps, but what about the joy of self-realization? Can *that* be found in an "imitation life?" Remember that projection of some type will obscure your understanding of the truths in the others' lives; your unconscious mind or emotions want to see them as heroes worthy of emulation, or as villains to be avoided and condemned.

Working to abide in personal truth seems to be a lifelong struggle for first cycle 4s. If you started life with a 4 lesson you may become disgusted at the quality of your unexamined life by middle age. Like Cinderella's sisters you may be trying to fit comfortably into the glass slipper of happiness with feet (a symbol for understandings/beliefs) swollen by too much copying, emulation and maladaptations to others' lifestyles. This is why many individuals find themselves in therapy at some point today. Socrates said, "The unexamined life is not worth living." It takes courage to look without blinking at the path we have already walked in life, but unless we *do* we'll continue to build our future on the shifting sands of illusions and untruth.

The 5 cycle: Above everything else, *expect* chaos. The function of a 5 cycle seems to be primarily one of **BREAKING UP RIGIDITY.** Most of us become rigid in some thought patterns or activities during life. We can deceive ourselves that this severity is holy, but you should consider that you may be blocking Spirit. Most of us cling tightly to old habits that *seem* to have sustained or protected us in earlier life. And perhaps they *did* protect and help us during some earlier phase of ego development and expansion. But we are creatures of Spirit, and not the earth. We are only sojourners here, and need to remember that.

5 cycles can involve us in frantic activity, perhaps travel, or they can seem to snare us in immobility. I have seen both happen in peoples' lives. Some individuals will move around continually during a 5 cycle. If 5 is one of your life lessons, your great energy can keep you continuously "involved," and may even appear to offer "meaning" to your life. But, genuine *understanding* may elude you. Each day may seem like another enemy that needs conquering, and you may lose sight of Spirit's workings in your life. **PATIENCE** is needed at these times. Remember that activity can be a form of addiction. The ego delights in such frenzy, as we "don't have the time" for reflection on where our busy-ness has taken us.

In 5 cycles we come to recognize our need to let some things work themselves out. A woman I know underwent three 5 cycles in a row, and most of that period involved a struggle with agoraphobia ("fear of open spaces"). Panic attacks ensued when she ventured very far from home. Her cognitive therapy seemed extremely slow, as she had to re-establish her former confidence and capability. One dimension of the 5 activity urges us to **LET GO AND LET GOD,** surrendering to a Higher Power because our ego-centered past has *not* brought us the peace and joy that "the little god" promised.

My personal experience with 5 cycles (as a 5 Destiny and 5 Atmosphere) is that, most often, the illusion of "something solid" lures our safety-seeking-self forward, but in truth, we are almost always being invited to "fly," as Patrick Overton urged. Everything in the known universe is in a state of flux, and we are being invited to see **CHANGE** as sometimes necessary and, in many instances, good. The 5 cycle offers us greater **FAITH** if we will dare to step out into the darkness of personal fear and ignorance.

As a first learning cycle 5 denotes "the addictive personality." At conferences, Bill and I have had individuals deny their addictive side, because they don't drink alcohol or do drugs. Nevertheless, in personal conversations with them, little time passes before some area of **RIGIDITY** or **COMPULSION** becomes obvious. Once the ego has found an apparent safety it does not want to relinquish what feels like *control* over life. It is interesting to find many of these individuals who cling tenaciously to "watch words," memorized formulae or Bible verses as their simplistic "truths." Genuine Truth is often very complex, however. Rather than granting them true liberation, reliance on the words or phrases alone leads them to **INFLEXIBILITY** and blindness to Spirit's abundant offerings. Rigidity becomes a seemingly virtuous idol. Expect to find difficulty in **ADAPTING** to new circumstances in those you know, who entered this life with a first learning cycle of E, N or W.

The 6 cycle: This cycle offers us greater exposure to **LOVE** in its many forms. A person may begin or end a **RELATIONSHIP** in a

6 cycle. I have known individuals who married in a 6, and a few years later divorced in a 6. It is always easier to look into others' lives than our own. What do you make of the fact that JonBenet Ramsey died in a 6 cycle? Was the issue her soul's "lovingness," or a lack thereof (in her or in someone else), or was it a need to face fear? Scripture tells us that a perfected form of LOVE will cast out **FEAR**, and one of the great fears in a superficial society is the illusion of not being loved.

The self-image or personality is the main focus of concern here, and you must know several individuals who seek LOVE neurotically. If love is not given to the self that we want others to accept, then we fear we might *have to* change! And that is fearsome, because then our old "*Me*" will die, won't it? Perfected love is at least as generous in giving as it is in seeking to receive. Yin and Yang must balance here too.

As noted earlier, **FORGIVENESS** is a necessary component in "loving." It may be equally important to forgive our own self as much as we forgive others. Some teachers suggest that we must learn to forgive ourselves *before* we are able to forgive others. We must acknowledge that we are imperfect (and in need of others' forgiveness) before we can honestly forgive the brokenness in those who have injured us in some way. I believe that "the slings and arrows of outrageous fortune" which Hamlet pondered *must* be one of the "final exams" before any of us leave the earth plane and rejoin The One. So many of the world's great lovers (e.g. Jesus of Nazareth) forgave their persecutors' ignorance in not knowing "what they do."

Though we all must work at relationships, the individual with **a first letter of F, O or X** seems to have "lovingness" as a major challenge. Some seem to need to "love less" and others appear to need to learn to "love more." Others need to replace some great hurt with giving. One woman I know had to learn to build more "selectivity" into her love life, looking more deeply into the *character* of her friends and lovers, before sharing her intimate life with them. President Franklin D. Roosevelt (working on a 6 in "Delano"), chose a similar challenge. I am fascinated by the many arenas of LOVE in which he was called to learn: with Eleanor, with his mother, his children, his mistress, and with the American people as a group.

The 7 cycle: Depending on where it occurs in the person's name, 7 can represent a time of great potential **SERVICE** to others, or a time in which an inflated ego must face **HUMILIATION**. 7, as an initiation to the "Thee" triad, leads the soul into experiences of genuine **HUMILITY**. This exercise cannot be just a pose, affectation or mental exercise, because the humble life must be *lived honestly and deeply.* If we attempt to **SERVE** others because *someone else* says it is right, or because we seek to impress others, we will eventually be unable to follow through on it. Our heart must be deeply involved in the activity. Anger or resentments *must* spring up in the person who is serving others for some ego reason (e.g. hope of thanks or acclaim). SERVICE must be freely given to the indwelling Spirit in others. We need to give because God or the universe has given to us.

A 7 first cycle suggests a life of HUMILITY, and I have found many proud individuals born with G, P or Y on the front of their given name. It seems that the soul selects very humbling circumstances or surroundings for the birth of some individuals. I know an individual whom I suspect of being a royal personage in a former life, born this time into a poor, working-class family, where every penny had to be accounted for. On top of this HUMBLE beginning, she has taken some real "shots" in this life, causing her to lessen the strong personal pride of early life.

If talented or gifted individuals take up The Way of Service, many times they unconsciously seem to aim at avoiding future false pride and/or haughtiness. Perhaps you have seen such strong personalities "brought down a peg" over the course of a lifetime. St. Francis of Assisi (a 7 name) is my personal hero in this regard. A first cycle of 7 seems to involve a spiritual "chastening" which, if we will accept it, can only make us stronger in The Kingdom.

The 8 cycle: When you encounter an 8 cycle of H, Q or Z your soul wants you to face some apparent lack in life, or to work more strongly in groups. Recall, please, that in 8 we are to discover that we *do* have **ENOUGH** in our life for this moment. If you are not on a path of self-inquiry or spirituality, you may continually be burdened with sensations of **DEPRIVATION** in an affluent society. The more you struggle to "get yours," the greater is your pain at "not making it." Your pain indicates that this goal is flawed.

There may be times when (in institutional or organizational jobs) you can actually find *proof* that people *are* out to "get you." There can be clear examples of superiors actively dismissing or disrespecting you. You can suffer pay decreases, lessened authority, burdensome responsibilities without adequate compensation, or be passed over for promotion. It can seem obvious that you are headed into some disaster. However, this crisis may be almost entirely the ego's self-protective lie. You have failed to understand some principle of The Kingdom. You may have unused talents or have failed to apply your hunches. There can be things you know you *might* do (get further training or education, for instance) but consciously avoid doing so, out of fear of some imagined consequences ("I'd have to totally rearrange my life!"). On one level you may understand the new path offers a cure for your unhappiness. However, your flawed self-image immobilizes you. Cayce said that if given "more" at this stage you would be unable to use it, and would only waste it. What we need to do in such dilemmas is make sure we are using *every* resource available to us. "Use what you have, then more will be given!" was his remedy. Finding that heaven has been hidden away inside you, just awaiting a changed consciousness, can help in rearranging your values.

A first cycle 8 seems to offer us much success in working as "catalysts" in large companies or organizations. H, Q or Z on the front of a name stresses our innate need to learn and practice **COMPROMISE** and **COOPERATION**. We need groups if we are to gain this experience. Compromise comes hardest when our opponents don't seem worthy of our gift of compromise. Perhaps you will find yourself working on judgmentalism at this spot.

In very competitive organizations, where workers struggle to gain even the smallest "edge" on co-workers, it is not a normal tendency to want to honor others' ideas or opinions. It is not normal for an insecure person to sacrifice some personal ambition so that Something Bigger can happen. All the more reason to resist the illusions of this world and light the inner fires of sacrifice. Remember one of the myths in 8: Spirit does not often operate by the apparent rules of this material world; it is moving you toward **GENEROSITY**. Remember the idea that we will take into the next world only what we have surrendered or given away. The person whose given name begins with 8 would do well to be a facilitator or networker in whatever endeavor they are involved with. This does not mean that (s)he should totally extinguish personal talents or viewpoints. After all, we are obliged to give from our talents and abilities, and not keep silent about our earnest observations. But finding common cause with others will likely yield this person much more happiness than grief.

The 9 cycle: Time for an **ENDING** of some sort. If you are a "retentive" type of person, you won't want to say goodbye to any one or any thing, even old habits that you know are negative ones. The energies of a 9 cycle offer us a chance at renewal, but more often *seem* to be depriving us of some "treasure" instead. The ego wants to keep all its options open, and hates to foreclose *any* choice. However, our lives can become very cumbersome and messy if we don't do an "inventory reduction" from time to time, eliminating those items that no longer serve our spiritual needs. If we are not connected to our spiritual source, it is hard to discern what our true needs *are*. Likely, we then suffer a deep sense of loss when necessity forces us to prune the weeds surrounding our ego castle.

9 cycles may appear in your life as great **ELIMINATION** garage sales or lawn sales. With one exception. We cannot say, "I'll give up this or that if you meet my price." Take what has become superfluous in your life and *throw it out*–it's house-cleaning time! Don't even bargain with the universe or set a price on the riddance. Too

often, our persona is unable to discriminate what its baggage is, or it just doesn't *want* to let go. So the Higher Self takes the initiative and forces a **PURIFICATION**.

You may have to say goodbye to a loved one who is dying or moving away during a 9 cycle. In the first 9 cycle of our life, I believe, we face some karmic bill that is presented for payment. On the level of soul consciousness, the decision has already been made before birth to "settle the debt." But usually, the conscious mind (through which our ego operates) rejects the opportunity or necessity. Ego will usually try to avoid such incidents if they are avoidable. One thing for sure: our dreams will have already warned us what is coming. Prepare to have old attachments **BROKEN** in 9 cycles.

I have found an extremely high incidence of abuse among females who have a 9 cycle in the first 16 years of life; much of it is sexual or physical abuse. It may occur just as often among males, though the effects may be less-readily seen. And, again sad to say, so much of this abuse (to the youngsters) seems to take place within their family–the people who theoretically should be the child's protectors. It should be understood, however, that what hurts people can vary from individual to individual. In a 9 cycle some part of our personality seems to get broken. At its very best, a 9 cycle leads us not just to being broken but also to having our hearts *broken open* so that we are filled with compassion and understanding for others who suffer.

A first cycle I or R seems to indicate a life that is dedicated (on the soul level, primarily) to **TRANSFORMATION** or **ATONE-MENT**. This can be very difficult if you are attempting to love and raise such an individual. For example, it is hard for a parent to watch a child "take his/her lumps" in life. But many times the evening out takes place away from the parent's view or control. Perhaps the best coping skill such a parent can teach (or model through personal behavior) is the popular "making of lemonade from life's lemons." Mythically the soul is trying to reach for **AT-ONE-MENT** with a Power greater than itself. Teachers or parents who use hard times as an occasion to blame, condemn or demonize those through whom the hurt has come, deprive the child or young person of the healing they will require. Such guidance can only foster a continuation of "victim" thinking or scapegoating. Remember that the mythical function of a 9 cycle and 9 first letter is to encourage the individual to "rise from the ashes." **RESURRECTION** is the positive reaction to what has seemed to be "death."

Before we leave this chapter let's take one more look at the **numbers missing in the birth name**, as this can yield another dimension to your personal myth. Various numerologists and different cultural groups throughout the world attribute a "male-ness" or "female-ness" to numbers, depending on whether these are odd or even. The Japanese, for example, consider odd numbers to be "strong or masculine," while the even numbers are dealt with as "weak or feminine." If you have worked with the concept of Yang and Yin, however, you understand that both qualities are necessary if you are to achieve wholeness.

Take a look at those numbers missing in your birth name. In this search, I prefer to use the Chinese words *yang* and *yin*, instead of *masculine* or *feminine*. The latter words tend to threaten peoples' self-image or personal myth. If more of these numbers are Yang (odd numbers: 1,3,5,7,and 9), or *forceful*, it is suggested that you have failed to be direct or assertive enough in past lives. Now you must work toward a better balance. If more of them are Yin (even numbers: 2,4,6,and 8), work with the myth that you may not have been "feeling" or "caring" enough in past lives. It does not matter if your gender is male or female. I have noted individuals who are male by gender in the present life, (as with myself) and who need to become more Yin in this life's activity. Other men can discover, by this process, a need to be more Yang. The same discoveries are available to women. Your gender in this life may dictate a great amount of *what* you do, but the choice of *how* you do it, is entirely yours.

Souls are drawn to various genders to assist their development of greater wholeness. It is my understanding that a soul will choose to live out a series of male lives, then some female ones, seeking the strengths and wisdom in each in order to be balanced. In Heaven we don't need genders. Considering the cultural values in the nation of your birth, some attributes (of which sexual identity is but *one*) offer a greater opportunity for growth. This is another reason to have a strong, affirming personal myth that you *use* daily. If you are inclined to let a spiritually neutral, asleep society define you as "good" or "bad" you will continually be dependent on the approval of others. You risk being unable to develop a strong "center" or the "you" that the your soul is reaching for.

If you are threatened (as some males are) by the suggestion that your Yin side needs strengthening, try working more with waiting and listening (not just hearing). Men who have learned to nourish and nurture others, especially the young, can offer wonderful role models to girls and boys alike. Allow your feelings and intuitions to emerge, accepting that whatever emotions you have *are* appropriate because they are uniquely yours. If these emotions make your life chaotic, get some help with them. Most therapists have a clearer view of what is "normal" than does the man on the street.

Fewer American women, after a century of feminism, seem to be threatened by the suggestion that they need to enhance their Yang qualities. However, there are many ethnic subcultures in this nation where the Yang woman can have a very difficult time.

If you are missing no numbers, assume that your soul is seeking a wide variety of opportunities, and that you need to be versatile in approaching life. Mythically you have had adequate experience in each of the nine number fields to successfully pursue growth in each. You are not necessarily "better" than your neighbor who is missing three or four lessons. In fact, you may be more *obligated* to pursue personal growth than they.

Afterword

Following NINE is TEN, representing the renewed self, the one who has stayed the course and completed a cycle in the process of Return. Wherever TEN appears as a total (as you reduce numbers to single digits in composing your chart) pause and consider how far you may have already come in your return to The Source, the Ancient of Days. Persevere in your struggle to live LOVE as well as you can, for as long as your opportunity to live a physical life remains. Sufi master Hazrat Inayat Khan has written:[1]

> *Earthly pleasures are the shadows of happiness, because of their transitoriness. True happiness is in love, which is the stream that springs from one's soul; and he who will allow this stream to run continually in all conditions of life, in all situations, however difficult, will have a happiness which truly belongs to him, whose source is not without, but within.*

---

[1] Hazrat Inayat Khan, <u>The Complete Sayings of Hazrat Inayat Khan,</u> 1991, New Lebanon, NY, Omega Publications, p. 222   "Reprinted by permission."

Appendix A
Cycles Calculation Chart

The numbers in this chart represent the age at which cycles conclude. If you have less than ten, or more than 28, letters in your birth name, calculate the cycle length on your own. Divide the arbitrary length of life of 75 years by the number of letters in the full birth name.   The dividend number represents the length of each of your cycles. Remember the first age you will write in before the first letter of your name is 0, representing your age at birth.

10	11	12	13	14
7.5	6.82	6.25	5.77	5.36
15	13.6	12.5	11.5	10.7
22.5	20.5	18.8	17.3	16.1
30	27.3	25	23.1	21.5
37.5	34.1	31.3	28.9	26.8
45	40.9	37/5	34.6	32/2
52.5	47.7	43.8	40.4	37.6
60	54.5	50	46.2	43
67.5	61.4	56.3	51.9	48.3
75	68.2	62.5	57.7	53.7
	75	68.8	63.5	59.1
		75	69.2	64.4
			75	69.8
				75

15	16	17	18	19
5	4.69	4.41	4.17	3.95
10	9.4	8.8	8.3	7.9
15	14.1	13.2	12.5	11.8
20	18.8	17.6	16.7	15.8
25	23.4	22.1	20.8	19.7
30	28.1	26.5	25	23.7
35	32.8	30.9	29.2	27.6
40	37.5	35.3	33.3	31.6
45	42.2	39.7	37.5	35.5
50	46.9	44.1	41.7	39.5
55	51.6	48.5	45.8	43.4
60	56.3	52.9	50	47.4
65	61	57.3	54.2	51.3
70	65.6	61.7	58.3	55.3
75	70.6	66.7	63.2	60
	75	70.8	67.1	63.8
		75	71	67.5
			75	71.3
				75

20	21	22	23	24
3.75	3.57	3.41	3.26	3.13
7.5	7.14	6.82	6.5	6.3
11.3	10.7	10.2	9.8	9.4
15	14.3	13.6	13	12.5
18.8	17.9	17	16.3	15.6
22.5	21.4	20.5	19.6	18.8
26.3	25	23.9	22.8	21.9
30	28.6	27.3	26.1	25
33.8	32.1	30.7	29.3	28.2
37.5	35.7	34.1	32.6	31.3
41.3	39.3	37.5	35.9	34.4
45	42.8	40.1	39.1	37.6
48.8	46.4	44.3	42.3	40.7
52.5	50	47.7	45.6	43.8
56.3	53.6	51.1	48.9	46.9
60	57.1	54.5	52.2	50.1
63.8	61	58	55.4	53.2
67.5	63.4	61.4	58.7	56.3
71.3	67.8	64.8	61.9	59.5
75	71.4	68.2	65.2	62.6
	75	71.6	68.5	65.7
		75	71.7	68.9
			75	72
				75

25	26	27	28
3	2.88	2.78	2.68
6	5.8	5.6	5.4
9	8.7	8.3	8
12	11.6	11.1	10.7
15	14.4	13.9	13.4
18	17.3	16.7	16.1
21	20.2	19.4	18.8
24	23	22.2	21.4
27	25.9	25	24.1
30	28.8	27.8	26.8
33	31.7	30.6	29.5
36	34.6	33.3	32.2
39	37.4	36.1	34.8
42	40.3	38.9	37.5
45	43.2	41.7	40.2
48	46.1	44.4	42.9
51	49	47.2	45.6
54	51.8	50	48.2
57	54.7	52.8	51
60	57.6	55.6	53.6
63	60.5	58.3	56.3
66	63.4	61.1	59
69	66.2	63.9	61.3
72	69.1	66.7	64.3
75	72	69.4	67
	75	72.2	69.7
		75	72.4
			75

Appendix B

The Universal Law

Revealed to people of good will in all the world's religions throughout time

CONFUCIANISM

What you donít want done to yourself, donít do to others.

6th Century B.C.

BUDDHISM

Hurt not others with that which pains thyself.

5th Century B.C.

JAINISM

In happiness and suffering, in joy and grief, we should regard all creatures as we regard our own self, and should therefore refrain from inflicting uupon others such injury as would appear undesirable to us if inflicted upon ourselves.

5th Century B.C.

ZOROASTRIANISM

Do not do unto others all that which is not well for oneself.

5th Century B.C.

CLASSICAL PAGANISM

May I do to others as I would that they should do unto me.

Plato-4th Century B.C.

HINDUISM

Do naught to others which, if done to thee, would cause thee pain.

Mahabharata-3rd Century B.C.

JUDAISM

What is hateful to yourself, donít do to your fellow man.

Rabbi Hillel-1st Century B.C.

CHRISTIANITY

Whatsoever ye would that men should do to you, do ye even so to them.

Jesus-1st Century A.D.

ISLAM

Let none of you treat his brother in a way he himself would dislike to be treated.

5th Century A.D.

SIKHISM

Treat others as thou wouldst be treated thyself.

16th Century A.D.

BAHAI

Choose thou for others what thou choosest for thyself.

19th Century A.D.

Lesson Keywords

1
Leader
Teacher
Pioneer
Innovator
One of a kind
Unity
Oneness
Isolation
Aloneness
Self-esteem
Self image
Identity
Initiation
Beginnings
Stand up
Egotism
Selfishness
Allegiance

2
Choices
Decisions
Differentiation
Discrimination
Alienation
Appearances
Illusions
Fence-sitting

11/2
Spiritual choices
Spiritual selectivity
Selflessness
Polarization
Tolerance
"the other"
Light/Darkness
"easy way"
Karma
Golden Rule

3
Body/Mind/Spirit
Diet
Emotions
Balance
Integration
Harmony
Stability
Vulnerability
Boundaries
Healing

4
Honesty
Self-honesty
Self discipline
Self acceptance
Self-study
Don't compare
Integrity
Truth
the "four sins"
Accountability
Dependability
Reliability
Trustworthiness

22/4
Inferiority
Ineptness
Laziness
Simplicity
Order
Approval seeking
Spiritual
    acceptance
Self-indulgence

5
Control
Adapting
Change
Patience
Will
Disobedience
Rebelliousness
Rigidity
Compulsions
Addictions
Fixations
Obsessions
Holding on
Perseverence
Expectancy
Listening
Waiting
Surrender
Denial
Manipulating
Inflexibility
Dependencies
Reductionism
Constancy
Devotion
Faith

6
Love
Relationships
Charity
Possessiveness
Fear
Courage

7
Service
Humility
Humiliation
Pride

33/6
Unconditional love
Intimacy
Vulnerability
Forgiveness

8
Compromise
Cooperation
Limitation
Frustration
"Enough?"
Detachment
Generosity
Networking
Co-creating
Stewardship
Waste
Conservation
Reverence
Channel of blessings

44/8
Spiritual compromise
Spiritual cooperation
Popularity
Attachments
Release
Power
Liberation
Hope
Joy

9
Endings
Renewal
Transformation
Reorientation
Resurrection
Redirection
Repentance
Cleansing
Purification
The Phoenix
New
Consciousness

About the Author

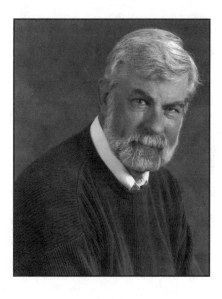

David J. Pitkin is a native of Corinth, NY, and has lived in Ballston Spa, NY, since 1971. In 1996 he retired after teaching Social Studies for almost 36 years in New York State public schools. Originally an American History teacher, he moved to teaching African & Asian Culture Studies to 9th Graders in 1968. He discovered how little western peoples (including himself) understand of social and spiritual beliefs in non-western cultures. As he taught others, he received an expanded education. In 1974, following a major illness, he began the study of parapsychology, and numerology in particular. The connections between religion and parapsychology have been of great interest to him. Over the years, he intuited his own unique numerology system which he has used, as David James Numerologist, in counseling seekers during the past quarter century. He holds Masters Degrees in Social Studies Education and Counseling Psychology. He has studied dream analysis with Dr. Montague Ullman and conducts a weekly dream study in his home. With his associate, Bill Getz, he is active in offering spiritual workshops and retreats throughout the United States and Canada.

Check your local bookstore, or order here:

Orderform

TO: Aurora Publications
P.O. Box 387
Ballston Spa, NY USA 12020

FROM: _____

(Your name)

_____

(Street address, PO Box number)

_____

(City, State, Country, Postal Code)

Please send me _____ copies of *Spiritual Numerology:*
Caring for Number One.

Price: $14.95 each...............................(Total for books) _____
NY State orders please include 7% sales tax.
All order shipped US Mail.
Include $3.50 Priority Mail postage
            or $2.00 regular postage ....(Total postage) _____

All remittances in US funds via check or money order
    payable to Aurora Publications

Total amount enclosed in this order............................._____